HUCKLEBERRY HEART:

THE BOYS OF HALLORAN AVENUE

―――

GENE NELSON ISOM

PublishAmerica
Baltimore

First printing

At the specific preference of the author, PublishAmerica allowed this work to remain exactly as the author intended, verbatim, without editorial input.

ISBN: 1-4241-3620-2
PUBLISHED BY PUBLISHAMERICA, LLLP
www.publishamerica.com
Baltimore

Printed in the United States of America

To my wife, Doris Ann
And my children
Jerry Nelson and Lora Kay

INTRODUCTION

I've heard it said that there is a book in every man. That may be true, but the work required to get it onto paper is exactly why every man does not write one.

The idea for this book came to me very slowly after speculating about the childhoods of my father and mother. My father's untimely death when I was in my teens left many questions that will never be answered about his youth and growing up around the coal mining areas of Ewing and Whittington, Illinois.

It may have been those unanswered questions about my father's youth that caused me to sit down and write about my childhood growing up around the community of Wood River, Illinois, to leave a legacy of my childhood to my children and grandchildren.

I never really anticipated the scope of this undertaking when I first began, or the many hours of labor that would be required. For every hour of writing, I spent two staring off into space, trying to recall my youth with as much accuracy as possible.

Although many hours of travel time went into collecting as much factual information as possible, there is no attempt at serious research for this endeavor for two reasons: First, the distance between the location about which I have written and where I presently reside made serious research rather difficult and expensive. Second, and probably the most important, it was my intention to write as I remember things to be without historical accuracy becoming a troublesome interference with the sweet memories of my youth that have mellowed with time and aged like good wine.

However, taking into account the mind's ability to exaggerate and embellish events of the past, and lest I give the reader the impression that this is a work of fiction, I must state that the events did happen when and where I've described them. There has been an honest attempt to corroborate the events about which I've written with those individuals involved whenever possible.

Although fifty plus years have passed since those wonderful carefree days of my childhood, my Huckleberry heart occasionally carries me back to the fields, woods, creeks and ponds of yesteryear that were such an important part of those formative years.

I will forever be grateful and feel fortunate that the first sixteen years of my life was spent in that mid-western environment on the banks of the Mississippi River in and around the community of Wood River, Illinois.

Come look with me inside this drawer, inside this box I've often seen, at the pictures, black and white, faces Proud, still, serene. I wish I knew the people, these Strangers in the box. Their names and all their Memories are lost among my socks.

I wonder what their lives were like, how did they spend Their days? What about their special times? I'll never Know their ways, if only someone had taken the time to Tell who, what, where or when, these faces of my Heritage would come to life again. Could this become the fate of pictures we take today?

The faces and the memories someday to be passed Away? Make time to save your stories, seize the Opportunity when it knocks, or someday you and yours Could be strangers in the box.

Author Unknown

ACKNOWLEDGEMENTS

I am grateful to the many people who gave me support and encouragement while writing this book. Despite the fact that this book is biographical in nature and made up of my memories, I found it necessary to rely on the help of many to refresh those memories from time to time.

First and foremost, I must give thanks and credit for the completion of this book to my wife, Doris Ann. It was her patience and constant support that made it possible. She served as my on-site editor and my best critic, giving positive and negative feedback.

Marvin, my brother, whose youth was so intertwined with mine, provided invaluable clarity to many of the events. My sister Norma, whose leg brace was responsible for the burning of the haystack, supplied the essential facts surrounding that and other stories. My sister Rita and brother Jack have helped by their retelling of our childhood escapades during the many family reunions and gatherings of the intervening years.

I am extremely grateful to Leila Horton Stokes, my patient and understanding manuscript editor and very dear friend, who has been a tremendous help and encouragement; whose timely intervention and help was so very crucial to the completion of this book.

Last but not least, I must thank the many who unknowingly gave support and impetus for this book while still in its initial stages. It's hard to place a value on their casual and complimentary comments, without which this book may never have been initiated or completed. To those who may or may not have known that they contributed, I can only say thank you.

TABLE OF CONTENTS

In the Beginning 15

The Chicken House 20

Hammond's Cow 23

Gambler's Luck 27

The Blistering Paddle 31

There She Blows! 36

The Barnstormers 42

Shots!!! 47

Gene and Marvin Become Employed 51

The Christmas That Almost Wasn't 53

Monty and Me 58

The Young Izaak Walton 65

Just a Little Slip 72

Learning to Swim 75

Interrupted Summer 79

Halloween Pranks 84

Baked Chicken, à la Indian Style 89

Hepcats and Jive-Talk 93

The Great Story Teller 97

Unknown American Hero 102

Resorting to Fisticuffs 107

Pearl Harbor 122

Mexican Stand Off...130

Fort Walnut 142

Hitchhiking to Olive Branch, Illinois 149

Runaways – To The Ozarks 163
Greyhound Bus to Brookport 175
The War Claims A Friend 185
The Conspiracy 194
At That Moment, I was Huck 201

Note 1: Rather than credit individual references in footnotes, all historical data contained within this book, concerning World War II, Rationing, War Posters, Comic Strip Characters, Scrap Drives, Wartime Songs, Radio Serials, Jive Talk, Zoot Suits, Hollywood Movies, and other historical data, were heavily based on "The Fabulous Century – Volume IV & V, 1930-1950, By – Editor of Time Life Books" © 1969."

Note 2: Much of the historical data concerning Wood River, the Wood River Swimming Pool, The Round House and Park, Schools, Local Heroes of The War, came from "The History of Wood River, Illinois, Diamond Jubilee Edition" © 1985

CHAPTER I

In the Beginning

I was driving north on U.S. 111, just south of what is called the Cahokia Diversion Channel, located about one-half mile south of Roxana, Illinois.

As I grew nearer my pulse quickened as my mind raced back to a period of time when life was much slower and a lot more predictable. In fact it was a time even before the highway on which I was traveling existed.

As I crossed the bridge I couldn't resist the temptation to stop. I got out of my car and crossed over and looked down, down and back into the past.

The year was 1942 as my mind recalled images of three young boys, ages 12 through 14, drifting by in an old rowboat they had found and painstakingly painted in black camouflage. This they had done in preparation for their planned adventure down the mighty Mississippi River to New Orleans. There were probably few young boys who grew up on the Mississippi in those days who didn't dream the adventures of Huckleberry Finn and Tom Sawyer. I'm sure there are a few still having that dream today.

I could have lingered there a while but the heavy traffic vibrating the bridge kept jarring me back to the present and their passing so close was doing little for my feeling of security.

Once back in my car, I eased out into the traffic and continued on north, and within a minute or so I was abreast of South Roxana. Glancing up to the right, I could almost see the house where we once lived, on Melrose Avenue. That was a long time ago. The year was 1936, but my visit there would have to wait its proper turn.

You see, the year is presently 1990 and this was to be a sentimental journey back to the place of my birth, my boyhood, the land that nurtured me

15

into manhood at a very young age. As I would later come to realize, it was this area and its mid-western environment that was to mold and instill in me values that to this day guide my life.

It was my intention to revisit all the locations that as a young boy were so much a vital part of my life. I wanted to revisit each house that we had lived in, each school that I had attended, each playground, the fields, creeks, woods, and especially the Wood River swimming pool where I had learned to swim and spent so many long hot summer days.

I wanted to recapture those long ago forgotten moments and events, memories that had long since faded and eroded with time.

*   *   *

Continuing on a short distance, I caught a faint but very distinct odor. It was a smell that has become as much a part of the area as the refineries themselves. It was a smell that would immediately let me know, on the few occasions when I was away for a period of time, that I was almost home. I was presently experiencing that same feeling of excitement that I had known so many years ago.

The smell of petroleum continued to increase along with my anticipation as I drove past the main entrance to the Shell Oil Refinery. This was the place my father had worked as a pipe fitter from the early 1920s through the 1940s.

I could instantly see that the main entrance had changed considerably since last I had passed this way. The brick guardhouse that had stood in the center was no longer there. The neat row of well maintained brick homes with their manicured terraced lawns were gone. Other changes had taken place also, presenting a barren and sterile appearance. I'm sure these changes were for the purposes of economy or, so-called progress; even so, the effect upon me was somewhat depressing. A short distance later the road bore to the right and now had become Central Avenue. I immediately recognized the old firehouse coming up on the right and eased over and stopped in front. This is it, the town of my birth, where for me it all started – Roxana, Illinois.

Sitting there in my car looking at the old rather run down building, I couldn't keep my mind from racing back to a time when my brother Marvin, cousin Tommy and I were walking by this fire station when an incident occurred that I've never forgotten.

To sit and watch the firemen going about their many duties was an exciting pastime for first and second graders in 1935. I recently put that incident into verse.

The Fire Truck

Three young boys all standing in awe,
Watching with fascination and gaping jaw,
The busy firemen going about their jobs,
Cleaning, fixing, and polishing knobs,
Making the fire engine look real keen,
It was the biggest these boys had seen.
When of a sudden the siren screams,
The firemen all scurry in practiced teams,
The three boys hurriedly scatter in haste,
Knowing too well there's no time to waste.
The big truck belched smoke and fire,
While leaving the station with squealing tire.
With firemen aligned hanging to the rack,
Their coattails standing straight out in back.
Away it goes with siren and bells,
The young boys chasing with whoops and
Yells. They were running like lickety-split,
Giving their all to catch up with it.
What red-blooded boy wouldn't try his luck,
To catch up with a passing fire truck.
Running onward for two blocks or more,
Catching this fire truck was to be quite a chore.
The young boys slowed to trot then a walk,
Then finally stopped without any talk.
They silently stood milling around,
For the fire truck now was way out of sound.
They then did turn with disappointed groans,
Heads held low they slowly walked back home.

*   *   *

While driving up Central Avenue, I was alert for any signs of familiarity. So many changes had taken place since this was so much a part of my everyday activity. This area back then was as natural to me as breathing.

Houses now stood where as boys we played in empty lots. As I passed

Fourth Street, I couldn't help but look to the left to the house in which we once lived for four years, between 1931 and 1935. I was very anxious to turn there and look, but I knew this would be my next stop, so I continued on up Central Avenue. Upon approaching Second Street, I slowed and made a right turn, then eased on up the street toward Chaffer Avenue. As I approached the fourth house on the right from the corner, I stopped.

This spot is where the house in which I was born stood. It was almost directly across the street from the house where Marvin, my brother, was born only eighteen months earlier.

The house is no longer there. It was a small shotgun house that had been replaced some years earlier. It was where it all started for me on the morning of September 5th, 1929. I came kicking and squalling into this world, weighing in at nine pounds and three ounces.

The world has never been the same. My arrival upon the scene had such a devastating effect upon the country, that within just a few days, the economic structure of this nation literally crumbled. It took twelve years and a world war before it was to recover.

All kidding aside, the economic conditions of the 1930s were unparalleled in the history of this country, and regardless of what they say, I refuse to take blame and I don't think anyone else knows either. The so-called experts have been arguing over who or what caused the depression for sixty years and still can't agree.

Although life was rough in the 1930s, some areas had it a lot worse than others. The Roxana-Wood River area had the support of two major oil refineries to lessen the impact.

My father was a pipe fitter for the Shell Oil Refinery and therefore had steady employment during the depression years.

During the beginning of this period, there were only four in the family. My father, John Nelson Isom, my mother, Dorothy Mildred, (maiden name Irey) my brother, Marvin James, and myself, Gene Nelson.

There would be three additions to the family within the next four years. My sisters, Rita Lee and Norma Fern were born in 1931 and 33, respectively. The seventh member was my youngest brother, Jack Ronald, born in 1934. This completed our family of seven.

There isn't much more to say about Second Street. Everything that occurred there was before I was old enough to remember. It wasn't until we moved to Fourth Street in 1931, that my life started coming together as I remember it.

Because there was really no reason to remain at this location, I started the car and eased on up to the corner and turned right onto Chaffer Avenue. I continued south two blocks and turned right on Fourth Street. Crossing Central Avenue, I pulled up and stopped about one hundred feet on the right in front of house number 114.

Chapter II

The Chicken House

As a toddler on Fourth Street, there was nothing to do but be just that, and to grow. There were no responsibilities to clutter my daily activity of play, except the rules and guidelines that I'm sure my mother laid down, as all mothers do. My world at the time consisted of one city block. My circle of acquaintances was mainly my immediate family and six or seven other kids near my age who lived within that one block.

Marvin, my brother, although only eighteen months older than I, seemed so much wiser for his years. He was my leader, advisor, and hero, and I can honestly say he still is today.

It was Marvin's cool logic and guidance that usually kept us out of harm's way. He was alert to trouble and always seemed to know just how far we could go without getting hurt or into trouble. He generally knew how to do something and in most cases it was he who decided what we would do.

One may get the impression that I've described a domineering know-it-all. This was not the case. Marvin had a quiet manner and congenial personality. His natural leadership was recognized and accepted by the kids with whom we played. This held true on up through our teenage years.

Lest I've given the reader the impression that he was infallible, hold on! Although in most cases his judgment was usually sound there were a few times when it failed him, and when it did, it was a whopper.

One particular time was while we were playing with two of our friends who lived on the corner of Fourth Street and Central Avenue. Their names were Billy and Jackie Dale. At that time there was a chicken house located in their back yard where the little one-car garage now stands. The chicken house was no longer being used, but still contained the nests filled with straw. This is where we were playing when Marvin's good judgment let us down.

HUCKLEBERRY HEART:
THE BOYS OF HALLORAN AVENUE

On this occasion while the four of us were playing in the chicken house, one of us, I'm no longer sure who it was, came up with a box of matches. You know how it is with boys and matches. They are drawn to them like a moth to a flame. Their parents have told them how dangerous it is and that they will get burned, but the fascination with fire at that age is overwhelming, and we were no different.

Marvin, sure we had the situation well in hand, decided we would make a small fire in the chicken house, well out of sight of prying eyes, especially those who for some strange reason always had objections to kids having fun.

There was a large brown gallon jug setting in the corner full of some type of liquid we thought to be water. With this on hand for any emergency that may arise, what could possible go wrong?

We played for some time, striking the matches and enjoying our new found freedom of playing with fire without adult supervision. After all, how often do four and five year olds get an opportunity like this?

It was inevitable I suppose, with four young eager boys, each trying to do their thing, that disaster was bound to happen. Now I don't want to point my finger, but I do believe it was the cool one that set the nest on fire.

During the first few seconds as the flames leaped upward and appeared to be getting out of control, there was no panic. However, shortly thereafter, it became apparent that patting it with our hands, or trying to smother it with more straw was not the answer.

In another moment thick white smoke was bellowing up and across the ceiling. By this time panic had definitely set in. We were jumping around in confusion when I remembered the jug setting in the corner. Picking it up, I handed it to Marvin, who edged up as close to the burning nest as he dared and doused it with the liquid in the jug. When the liquid hit the flames, the nest literally exploded with a "whoomp" sound and a huge fireball rose to the ceiling.

The four of us scattered like a covey of quail. Billy and Jackie Dale headed for the back door to their house and Marvin and I took off lickety-split across Fourth Street to our house.

We're not sure what happened next or who called the fire department, but it seemed only minutes before they arrived. They came screeching around the corner with siren screaming and bells clanging, as Marvin and I peeked over the window sill of our front bedroom window.

We remained there, wide-eyed and terrified, until the fire had been extinguished and a couple of firemen started walking toward our house.

Terrified that we were surely going to jail, we dove under the bed and remained there until we were finally coaxed out by our mother, assuring us that we were not about to become jailbirds. She didn't, however, make any such promise not to tan our hides. At applying the switch, mom had no equal. Had we had a choice, jail or a good switching, I'm sure it would have been a hard decision to make.

Chapter III

Hammond's Cow

Life on Fourth Street in Roxana during the 1930's was a young kid's dream. Mom, though constantly home and hovering over her brood, did give us quite a bit of freedom to explore and grow.

The amount of freedom allotted us during those early years, I'm convinced, contributed much to the early independence that my brothers and I exercised when we grew into our teens. This may not necessarily have been for the best, although I wouldn't have taken anything for the adventures I've experienced. I would, however, try to find a way to squeeze in a few more of the really important things.

In those early years we rarely ventured more than a couple of blocks from home, with the exception of visiting our cousin, Tommy Lawrence who lived on Seventh Street. Our mothers being sisters and living in close proximity, created a close-knit relationship between our families. As cousins, we were inseparable in those early years. If Tommy wasn't at our house, we were at his.

*   *   *

Our sister Rita had now joined the family. She was born August 27, 1931, in Olive Branch, Illinois on the Lige Brown place on Sandy Ridge. Rita was the little lady of the family, always prim and proper. She naturally did the right thing. Rarely if ever, did she do anything that would even rate a scolding. She was very steady and never demonstrated the urge for wander-lust, as the rest of us did. To this day she is still the perfect little mother and grandmother.

Norma joined the family on July 19, 1933. She was born on Fourth Street in Roxana. With her arrival our family had rapidly grown to six. The children now consisted of two boys and two girls. The family was fortunate that our father had steady employment during that period. The depression was getting into full swing and a family the size of ours would have had a very hard time making ends meet otherwise.

With Norma's arrival, Marvin's life and mine took on some drastic changes. First off, Norma had a strong urge to roam. No sooner had she learned to walk, than she started wandering off. Marvin or I would have to go find her and bring her back home.

We knew a family named Hammond that lived on Chaffer Avenue, between Tydman and First Street that owned a cow. We often would buy milk from them. Evidently Norma had become very attached to that old cow, and took every opportunity to slip away and go visiting. Whenever this occurred, it meant that Marvin or I would have to go find her once more and bring her back home.

Mom, of course, would paddle her behind, but that did little to deter her. As they say today, "It failed to change her behavioral pattern." It appeared the fascination with that cow was stronger than the fear of punishment.

Mom eventually tried a makeshift harness, which she attached to a rope that was tied off at the other end to the porch. This tether gave her ample room to roam and play in the yard, yet limit her from going beyond the front sidewalk.

One day while playing in the front yard in this fashion, she managed to slip her bonds and make her getaway. Upon my noticing the empty harness lying in the yard, I ran through the front door yelling, "Mom! Mom! Norma has run away again!" Following Mom to the front yard, we looked up and down the street, but by then, she was well out of sight. Mom said to me, "Go get her son, you know where she's headed."

I took off up Fourth Street as fast as I could run, feeling proud that I was grown up enough to be trusted with this responsibility.

I ran on across Central Avenue and on down to Chaffer. As I rounded the corner at Chaffer, low and behold, there stood my gallivanting sister about one block ahead. As I ran toward her, my enthusiasm for this once proud assignment was waning rather rapidly. In fact, I stopped short about one half block from where she was standing, seriously debating whether to pretend I didn't know her and keep walking, or go back and get *her* mother to handle *this* job. After all, what six-year-old boy wanted to be seen by his friends, or anyone else for that matter, in such an embarrassing predicament?

You see, to my consternation and embarrassment, there stood my sister stark naked from the waist down. Somewhere along the way, she had managed to discard her clothing.

Grudgingly, unable to shirk my responsibility and with red face and head down, I pulled, sometimes dragging my little sister home as fast as I could.

This was not the last of Norma's sorties. However, they were not to last much longer. For fate was soon to raise it's ugly head and strike a blow far more severe than any possible disciplinary punishment.

Norma became ill one morning and developed a very high fever. It didn't take the doctor long before diagnosing her condition as the dreaded "P" word...Polio.

Polio was at epidemic proportions during the early 1930s. This was long before Doctor Jonas E. Salk. There really wasn't much anyone could do except to let it run its course, and of course pray, and believe me, there was a lot of praying going on around our house at that time. They must have been answered, because Norma survived, even though she would never run again. We were fortunate, as so many children who came down with this dreaded disease did not.

One aspect of this era in our country's history that is different today is the handling of communicable diseases. There were rather rigid laws governing control that today would be considered archaic. These laws I suppose were a holdover from the days before vaccines became prevalent; and also before individual rights took precedent above the rights of the public at large to be protected. Households with occupants infected with mumps, measles, chicken pox, or other like diseases were quarantined.

I remember on several occasions when the doctor had diagnosed such illnesses within our family. He was required to report it, and either he, or other health officials would put signs on both the front and back doors of the house.

The sign was dark red with "QUARANTINE" written in bold black letters across the middle and the nature of the illness penciled in. Once the sign was in place, no one was allowed to leave or enter the house.

I can still remember to this day that tap-tap-tap sound. After he finished at the front, all of us kids would run to the rear and wait for the tap-tap-tap on the back door.

When this occurred at our house, our father was required to remain away from home until the quarantine had been lifted. On such occasions he would bring groceries to the front porch, leave them, then back away. Mom would then go out and retrieve them. These quarantines lasted no more than five to seven days.

So it was in those days, but was it wrong to temporarily inconvenience a few for the many—the many that would not have survived otherwise.

CHAPTER IV

Gambler's Luck

July 4th, 1935 was the first Independence Day that I remember actually celebrating. That 4th was the first that I was directly and personally involved in setting off fireworks without adult supervision.

The day before, Mom gave Marvin and me fifty cents each to buy fireworks. Now I realize that by todays standard that may not sound like a lot of cash, but I can assure you that during the depression years, you could buy a lot of BANG for the buck. Fifty cents would purchase several packs of firecrackers, a couple boxes of sparklers, and a few roman candles.

Marvin and I took off for Harbke's store only a few blocks away on Central Avenue. We painstakingly made our selection with the assistance of the storekeeper, who I'm sure was Mr. Harpke. Although Marvin was an educated first grader, he like I, still needed a lot of help with the high finance involved.

After making our purchases we hurried home and went straight to our bedroom. Once there we excitedly placed our treasures neatly on the floor to admire. During the day and evening, we probably had our fire-works in and out of the sack at least a dozen times. The anticipation of the next morning was almost more than I could endure.

I remember waking early the next morning. The sun had barely risen when I jumped into my uniform of the day, bib overalls only, because shoes and shirts and any other articles of apparel were discarded on the first day of summer.

Grabbing my sack of fireworks and a box of farmer matches that I made sure to have handy, I took off running out the front door and on across the street to what was then an empty lot. Two houses are now located there.

With total disregard or consideration for anyone trying to get a few extra winks on a holiday morning, I set off my first firecracker. In the early morning quiet, it sounded like the whole world exploded. With my ears covered and standing about twenty feet away, it even startled me.

I expected any second to see everyone come pouring out of their houses, at least all the boys on the block. I was right. Marvin was the first, then within the next ten minutes or so we had five or six there.

Here again, we find not only the contrast between the control and laws governing fireworks in the 1930s compared to today, but also the way children were left to their own devices concerning the use of fireworks.

I can't help but wonder if all the governmental controls and restrictions, both at the local and federal levels of today, have really succeeded in reducing fires and personal injuries. Regardless, to suggest controlling such activity back then would have been considered down right un-American.

The field in which we set off our fireworks served as our playground. We spent most of our playtime in this field. It was here that we flew our kites, played marbles and dug our caves.

For some unexplained reason, kids had a thing about caves in those days. You could not walk an empty lot in the whole of the Roxana-Wood River area without finding these caves being used as forts, club- houses, or just plain open pits of every kind and description.

Some had wood covers; others had tin, or a combination, which also included weeds. I often thought that from the air they probably appeared as bomb craters.

*   *   *

It was while we were living on 4th Street in Roxana that Marvin had to have his tonsils removed. He was hospitalized for a couple of weeks at Barnes Hospital in St. Louis, Missouri. During his stay I was pretty much at a loss playing alone. Up to this time we were rarely separated. It was he who made sure I didn't stray too far from the line.

It was while he was away that I suddenly got the idea that I was a great marble player. Later on I did acquire a certain level of skill at the game, however, at five years old I was soon to find out that I wasn't nearly as good as I thought. There were a couple of kids on that block that were a little older and a whole lot better at the game than me.

When we played marbles, it was supposed to be for "Funs," not "Keeps." Mom had always told us that playing for keeps was the same as gambling, which of course everyone knew was a sin. I didn't want to sin of course, because at only five years old, I already knew where sinners ended up. But all the kids on the block were doing it. And after all, what boy didn't have at least one vice?

Marvin and I both had our own collection of marbles. We kept them in old coffee cans. My collection covered about three inches in the bottom of the can and Marvin's was close to being full.

My collection was made up of an assortment of just the run of the-mill types; Marvin's, on the other hand had been meticulously collected over a long period of time. Each one he considered a treasure, each a collector's item. He had lobsters, agates, we called them agees, beautiful pee-wees, and his choice taws, which of course were his shooters.

It wasn't too long before I had lost all my marbles playing keeps. Like all gamblers, I was sure I could recoup my losses if I just hung in there long enough. Like all gamblers, I was wrong.

Standing around the circle watching others play was not my idea of fun. The longer I had to stand idly by watching, the more tempting Marvin's big can of marbles just setting under the bed, became.

I was able to fight this temptation for a while, but eventually I convinced myself that borrowing just a few would do no harm. After all, upon winning I could always put them back – right?

About one-half can later I realized that I had really boo-booed bad. I had lost half of Marvin's marbles with absolutely no way to replace them. Putting just any marbles back in the can wouldn't work. Because of his familiarity with each, he would immediately recognize them as fakes.

It was only a couple of days before Marvin was to return home and I was going through torment trying to come to a solution to my dilemma. Eventually realizing there was none, I decided I would just have to throw myself upon his mercy.

I did, however, spend the next couple of days hoping upon hope, that someone, someway, somehow, would save me from the thrashing I knew was sure to come as soon as Marvin discovered my foul deed. I knew if he told Mom I would get a good switching. However, I was fairly confident that this was something he would handle himself, man to man, so to speak. During our adolescent years, Marvin or I, rarely if ever, ran to Mom or Dad for assistance in settling our disputes.

Time was not my ally. It only prolonged the inevitable and my dread. On the other hand I wasn't about to tell him. After all, there was always that long shot – a miracle.

Upon Marvin's return home it didn't take him long before discovering my misdeed. In fact, it was only a matter of hours before he went to look at his marbles. I can still hear today that outburst that reverberated throughout the house. I was sitting on the couch in the living room when I heard Marvin loudly shout, "OK! WHAT HAPPENED TO MY MARBLES?" I slowly tried to make myself invisible by scrunching down into the couch.

What happened next is not quite clear. My memory is rather foggy as to the actual events. I do recall receiving a rather severe tongue lashing by just about everyone in the family, which of course I justly deserved. Marvin never resorted to fisticuffs, which he was prone to do if duly provoked. However, there were many future occasions when he felt it necessary to remind me of my pilferage. I do recall at the time of trying to reverse the blame for leaving all that temptation in my way. I suppose at the age of five I was already starting to show a certain tendency toward liberalism that would eventually permeate our society.

There is a footnote to this story. Marvin did eventually rebuild his marble collection to some degree. However, after he was a young man and out on his own, our tomboy sister Norma and her friend Larry, decided Marvin's marbles made great slingshot ammunition. Marvin's once proud collection can now be found scattered over the hillsides, overlooking Pigeon Roost Hollow, in southern Illinois.

Chapter V

The Blistering Paddle

On October 3, 1934, Jack Ronald, the last to join our family was born at 114 Fourth Street, Roxana, Illinois. I remember this occasion very vividly. The day before, for some unexplained reason, Marvin and I were hustled off to Tommy's house. Now ordinarily there would be nothing unusual about this, except we usually had to ask.

Although Tommy had a full size bed in his bedroom, his baby crib was still in the room. On this particular night for some reason that I will never understand, we all three chose to sleep in the crib together. One five year old and two six year olds, jammed into that small crib with legs and arms tangled and dangling between the railing bars, was truly a sight to see. The misery of trying to sleep in such cramped quarters is one reason I remember it so well. Why one or more of us didn't go to the big bed I'll never understand.

The next morning, Aunt Wave came in to wake us and announce that Marvin and I have a baby brother. I thought what a strange thing to happen. I couldn't remember there being any discussion concerning an addition to the family.

Marvin and I returned home that afternoon and went into the bedroom where Mom was lying. Next to her was our baby brother Jack. While looking down at the puckered little thing I was very puzzled about the whole thing. I can never recall Mom being pregnant nor was I able at the time to reason the process out. At age five, the process of procreation was beyond my reasoning capabilities. It was a year later that I first heard the four-letter slang word for the sex act. And the result has forever been etched into my mind.

It was during one of the many occasions while playing with other boys that one of them, a little older and whose name will remain anonymous, told us that our mothers and fathers had to – BLANK – to get us. He of course used the four-letter slang word. He didn't however actually describe the act, which only left me more confused. Had he been more explicit, he would have saved me a very embarrassing moment.

Later while walking home I couldn't get what the boy had said off my mind. At the time I never realized his revelation was a taboo subject and was determined to ask Mom and Dad about it.

Because the summer that year was so hot, Mom and Dad moved the cook stove, table and chairs, to the basement, where it was much cooler for cooking and eating. It was where I found them as I entered and sat down on the stairs about half way down.

Dad was reading the paper at the table and Mom was at the stove preparing the evening meal. I sat there for a moment before blurting out, "Mom, did you and Dad have to – BLANK – to get me?" Dad's head bounced up from the paper and Mom's head jerked in my direction. The expressions on their faces were total shock that instantly told me I had asked the wrong question.

Dad started snickering and Mom's face became beet red. She yelled out "Where did you hear that?" Knowing I could possibly be in big trouble, without hesitation, I quickly snitched on the boy. Mom replied, "Don't you listen to him and what's more I don't want you playing with him, he's not a nice boy." I promised her I wouldn't and took off up the stairs and out the door as fast as I could go. That was the last said on the subject, but I would give anything today to know what was said after I left.

*   *   *

Marvin with his fertile imagination immediately started applying Jack, our baby brother, with nicknames. Some of the most common were: Fritz, Feard Notta, Forty Thousand, and Brono Hauptmann, of Lindberg kidnapping fame. Dad put a stop to that one.

Jack must have acquired some of his older brother's vivid imagination, because by the time he began to talk, he also became quite a storyteller.

He had an occasion to visit our grandfather's farm in Brookport, Illinois and the sight of all those cows and horses had an effect upon him because it wasn't long after his visit that he started telling everyone about his imaginary farm.

He would tell us all about his purple mooles, blue mooles and yellow mooles. He was unable to say mules. When he was asked where his farm is located, he would always reply with "Way far down the hill." No matter how many times you questioned him about his farm, his answers never varied.

*   *   *

1935 was a lot different than 1934 as far as I was concerned. The depression was still raging in most parts of the country. Brono Hauptman had been found guilty and sentenced to die for the kidnapping and murder of the Lindberg baby. Will Rogers and Wiley Post have been killed in an airplane crash in Alaska. Huey Long, governor of Louisiana had been assassinated, and worse yet, I had to start going to school in September.

Marvin and Tommy, one year older than I, already had one year behind them and were headed for the second grade. They had survived their "baptism of fire." They had "paid their dues."

As old veterans they took glee in scaring the living daylights out of me; telling me how mean the teachers were and how they looked for the least excuse to whip you.

The instrument of punishment, according to Marvin and Tommy was a long wooden paddle about one inch thick with lots of holes to increase the pain and cause blisters.

You see, a few days before school was to start I made a mistake of asking too many questions. It didn't take those two long before they realized my apprehension. This was a serious mistake on my part because they wouldn't let up on me and by the night before school was to start I was in a terrible state of mind. The thought and fear of getting my butt blistered by that paddle was all I could think of.

I finally went to Mom and told her what Marvin and Tommy had been telling me. She tried to reassure me that it wasn't true, that they were just teasing, but somehow it didn't relieve my anxiety.

The next morning I went through the routine of getting dressed for my first day of school. I can't remember what I wore but I'm sure it was bibbed overalls, a long sleeve shirt with a large collar, and of course shoes and socks because summer was now over.

I finished dressing as if I were a zombie. At the proper time Marvin and I, with our lunches in hand, went out the door and down to the corner of Fourth and Central to wait for Tommy. He would come up from Seventh Street and then we would continue on to school together.

Marvin and I had done this very same thing the year before, except then, Tommy and Marvin walked on to school without me. I could only stand there and watch them go, feeling lonely and lost. This time I would have liked nothing better than to do just that.

As we walked up Central Avenue toward school Marvin and Tommy walked ahead carrying on a casual conversation, while I tagged along behind. The thought occurred to me that they were taking this awful casually for someone about to get beat with a blistering paddle.

The first day of school was uneventful, except for my own fear. When I first entered the school building I must have looked like a criminal that had just heard the prison doors slam shut.

Every adult that I passed in the hallway was given a wide berth. After what Marvin and Tommy had told me, I wasn't about to bring notice to myself. "Out of sight out of mind." And "out of mind out of trouble," hopefully.

I'm not sure how I found my classroom, only that I was there and so far, so good. The school started with introductions and the "Pledge of Allegiance" to the flag. The rest of that first day is a blank.

All I can remember about the day is that it finally ended. I can remember running home as fast as I could, not waiting for Marvin or Tommy, just happy that I had lived through it without being paddled. I guess that set the stage for my future relationship with school, because I never did get the hang of it.

On the way home I was beginning to understand how foolish my fears had been. I began to realize that if what Marvin and Tommy had been telling me was true, they would have come home the previous year beat up every day, because if there were two that deserved a blistering, those two did.

The rest of the school year wasn't too bad. It didn't take me long to realize however, that my two favorite subjects were *recess* and *lunch*. My heart wasn't in the classroom. After all that was pretty dull stuff after spending all my free time flying kites, playing marbles, or playing with frogs, bugs, insects, and especially harnessing July flies to match boxes and pretending they were horses, or making furrows in the ground with a spoon, pretending that I was a farmer plowing my field. This was my element and I could allow my imagination to run wild.

Recess was really great. I was back doing what I did best; playing. I would run from swing to the teeter-totter, to the merry-go-round; spend a few minutes on each, then make my rounds again. But of course, time allotted for recess was always too short. I would no sooner get started on something exciting, than the bell signaling the end of recess would ring.

Lunchtime was also great. If I'm not mistaken we were allotted a whole hour for lunch. Lunches were much different back then. No hot school lunches. We either went home for lunch, ate out, or brought our lunch in paper sacks or folded in newspaper and tied with string. The latter was the method that Mom usually used. It was a matter of utility and economy. Newspaper was plentiful, while paper sacks were expensive or otherwise scarce. Some of the kids brought their lunches to school in metal pails or lunch boxes.

Our lunches usually contained one or two sandwiches wrapped in wax paper, consisting of a combination of peanut butter and jelly, or plain butter and jelly, and often some homemade cookies. They also included an apple, orange, or banana when available. If the sandwiches contained meat, it would usually be meatloaf or sausage. Rarely, if ever, did they contain processed lunchmeat. It was a few years later before Mom started using lunchmeat on a more regular basis.

Occasionally we would get a treat. Mom would give us lunch money to eat out. There was a small store just about a block from school on Central Avenue. It had a soda fountain and grill. The proprietor had a school lunch special, made up of a small bowl of chili, a hamburger and soda pop.

To buy these three items for fifteen cents sounds ridiculous compared to today's prices, but you must keep in mind that this was during the peak of the depression and fifteen cents was a lot of money. Only three years earlier, in 1933, the dollar had been devalued to 59.09 cents and the gold standard was set at thirty-five dollars per ounce.

*   *   *

As young children, our perception of time was somewhat distorted, or in most cases irrelevant. We didn't really understand time, nor in most cases did we care; that was, until we were having fun, then it became too fast, and if not, it became much too slow.

It was at the end of my first summer break, just before starting into the second grade, that this was made evident to me. Marvin pointed out to me that we only had three months of summer vacation, after being required to attend school for nine. What outrage and indignation I felt for this totally unfair treatment. Up to that time I had assumed the year was divided equally. I couldn't understand how grown-ups could think that school was more important than summer vacation.

Chapter VI

There She Blows!

1936 and 1937 were years with much history. Roosevelt was now President; elected in 1936 by a landslide, with over five hundred electoral votes. King George V had died and Edward the VIII abdicated the throne to wed a commoner. The lighter-than-air Airship, the Hindenburg, had exploded and burned at Lakehurst, New Jersey, on May 7, 1937. Amelia Earhart was missing while on her global flight. Roosevelt was unsuccessful in his attempt to pack the Supreme Court by increasing the bench to fifteen. Remember – "A switch in time saved nine." King George VI was crowned in England and we moved from Fourth Street in Roxana to Melrose Street in South Roxana.

I sat in my car a few more minutes, taking a long last look at the house on Fourth Street; the house we had moved from more than fifty years earlier. I was impressed at how well the house appeared to be maintained. The front porch was now enclosed. When we lived here it was open with a banister railing.

Taking one last look, I then started the car and moved on down the slight grade (which seemed like a mountain back then) to the end of the street and turned left, heading south toward South Roxana.

As I drove, I looked up to the left and once again looked at the old fire station. I passed the Shell Refinery once more and soon came to the intersection of US 111 and Madison Road. This intersection did not exist when we moved to South Roxana. In 1937 the road just curved to the left and continued on eastward toward the small community of Wanda.

At the light I turned left onto Madison Road and continued a short distance before turning into the first street on the right. I pulled up and stopped in the middle of a small gravel parking area.

This lot was once used as a small switching yard for the railroad. There were several sets of tracks, which usually held a few freight and tank cars setting sidetracked.

This was a very busy and noisy place at that time, with the constant banging and clanking of railway cars, being coupled or uncoupled. With our house located less than two hundred feet away, we soon became accustomed to the acrid smell of coal smoke from the steam engines.

I can still hear the engineers giving their various signals. Some were long, some short, and others consisted of a series of short blasts.

I can remember lying in bed at night, hearing the trains in the distance. Their whistles would slowly grow louder, along with the clickety clack, clickety clack of the steel wheels striking the couplings in the rails. The sound would reach its peak as the train passed our house, and then slowly diminish as it continued on down the line toward Hartford. The lonesome sound of the whistle would slowly fade and soon be gone. I would lie there and wonder where it was heading and how far away it would be by morning.

Other sounds that went unnoticed during the day would be magnified at night. As I lay in my bed, I would hear the many sounds that were unique to the refinery so close by. There would be a variety of hissing sounds. Some were high pitched, others like a low growl, and whistles of various frequencies and volume.

As I sat there, I suddenly recalled an incident that had occurred on this very spot on which I was parked, some fifty-three years earlier. The railroad workers of the yard were always busy with some type of repair activity. Marvin and I, always curious, would take every opportunity to watch when we could.

It was while a crew was welding and cutting on some rails that Marvin and I edged up as close as we dared and sat down on a rail to watch. Either we had become a nuisance or the workers though they would have a little fun at our expense, because one of the men that was using a cutting torch, raised his shield, looked up at us and said, "Boys, if this thing ever makes a loud pop, you better run like hell because it's really getting ready to blow." He then flipped his shield back down and continued to cut the rail.

Marvin and I sat there wide eyed, not sure we wanted to be there, but, still not wanting to leave. Nothing happened for a while and we were just starting to feel at ease again, when all of a sudden there was a loud POP. All the men jumped straight up and one yelled loudly, "THERE SHE BLOWS!"

Talk about two boys scattering gravel…Marvin and I took off for home as fast as our short legs would move, believing any second we were going to be blown to smithereens. We didn't stop or look back until we had rounded the corner of our house. After huddling there for a few moments and nothing happened, we edged up to the corner of the house and peaked around. The workers were back to work as if nothing out of the ordinary had happened. We were not sure if a real crisis had existed, but I think we suspected that we had been had.

* * *

In 1937, South Roxana was much different than now. The population then was probably no more than five hundred. Today, in 1990, it is probably several thousand.

I noticed other major differences as well. The old school that served all grades from first through eighth was no longer there. It was located where the ballpark is now, between Smith and Roxana Avenues.

Another noticeable difference was the absence of the little four-by-four foot buildings that once aligned the alleyways directly behind each home. If you looked closely – well actually, you didn't have to look too close – you would have seen the well worn paths that ran straight from the back door of the house to the out house in the most direct line possible; a surveyor could not have done better.

At first, we found using these outdoor facilities very adventuresome. It didn't take long, however, before the novelty of this experience began to wane. During the day when the weather was good, it wasn't too bad. But, on most occasions the weather was too hot, too cold, too rainy, or too dark.

Nighttime was the worst, especially if it was raining or snowing. As young kids we were afraid to go in the dark alone. With five kids in the family, we were usually successful in enlisting the accompaniment of at least one other with the same urges, or thought it best to take advantage of the opportunity while they could. In case of absolute need there was always the chamber pot, kept handy for such emergencies. However, we only used the pot as a last resort, because whoever used it had the icky job of cleaning it the next day.

One other very memorable aspect of these outhouses was their attraction as Halloween targets. It was the custom of older boys on Halloween night to run up and down the alleys, turning over as many as they could. The next morning would find only those well anchored still standing upright.

The day after Halloween, many stories connected to the previous nights pranks started making the rounds. We would hear about the unlucky occupant, who while responding to nature's call, just happened to be inside at the time of the attack. Also, there was at least one story of poetic Justice; a story about the unlucky prankster who became careless while slipping around in the dark, and just happened to wander into a privy hole created by an earlier prankster.

*   *   *

Life at 108 Melrose Street in South Roxana in 1937 was fairly good to young impressionable eight and nine year old boys. There were adventures unlimited. We had Grassy Lake virtually outside our door. This lake by the way is no longer there. The Owl Patch was but a few blocks away at the end of Cemetery Road and just beyond that was the canal. The airport was just across Hedge Road, and the Shell Oil Refinery was just across the street from our house.

Grassy Lake received most of our attention, not only because of its proximity, but mainly because of the wildlife and adventure it provided. The swampy area came up just below Velma, Smith and Sinclair Streets and continued on west almost to Hartford. It was divided only by the railroad that ran on west to Hartford, which is now Madison Road. It stretched south all the way to the Cahokia Diversion Channel, which we referred to as the canal.

This was a few years before Route 111 and the many storage tanks that now fill this area. At that time Grassy Lake was made up of hundreds, perhaps even thousands of acres of cattail marshes with open patches of water, interconnected with winding shallow rivulets.

The depth of the water in these small connecting channels depended upon the season. At times, these channels would have but a few inches of water and we would wade them, being careful not to lose our balance on the smooth slick clay bottoms. We would walk with our arms outstretched, scooting our bare feet along the slick mud as if we were ice-skating.

During the hot summer months, these little canals would dry up and huge cracks would appear in the hard clay. Only the little lakes and deeper potholes would retain water throughout the hot dry summer months.

We used these sun-baked paths to wander throughout these cattail swamps. They would lead us from pothole to pothole; from one black willow thicket to another, which we referred to as oases.

Grassy Lake teemed with wildlife. Marvin, Tommy and I would travel throughout this area like nomadic Indians listening, observing and investigating everything that moved or made a noise.

There were literally hundreds of red-winged blackbird nests woven between the cattail reeds. Few were passed without receiving our thorough inspection. Still today, I have an instant flashback to my childhood in South Roxana and a warm nostalgic feeling each time I hear the warbling notes of a red-winged blackbird.

Another exciting inhabitant of the cattail thickets, although rarely seen, was what we called a prairie chicken. It was brown with a rather long slender neck resembling a Roadrunner. We were never really sure of its proper name. To flush one of these birds, or to find and inspect its nest, was considered the highlight of the daily excursion into this wild area.

The waters of Grassy Lake, especially toward the north end was unsuitable for fish. Because of the petroleum seepage from the storage tanks of Standard Oil, the water always smelled and tasted of oil. It was only toward the south end of the Grassy Lake area that we were able to catch catfish and sun perch.

The oily water, however, seemed to have no ill effects on the crawdads and turtles. In fact, they appeared to thrive on it, at least at the level of contamination present at that time.

At the end of Velma Street, down off the hill a short distance out in the cattails was a wooden pier. It didn't appear to be on any particular piece of property. It just stood out there all by itself. Marvin and I still speculate to this day as to its origin. It was rather old and may have belonged to an earlier homestead located at that site.

This old pier served us well. You could generally find one, two, or all three of us there fishing for crawdads, when not elsewhere engaged.

For some odd reason, crawdad fishing was a fascinating activity of which we rarely grew tired. They really served no useful purpose. We didn't eat them, although we did make an attempt once. Not knowing how to properly prepare and cook them, the experiment turned out very badly. The taste was very bland and of course oily.

Our method of catching crawdads was to lie on our stomachs, using a piece of string to which a bit of bacon rind was attached, then lowering the rind to the bottom and very patiently waiting, watching for any movement of the string. When movement was detected, we would very slowly lift the string with the crawdad holding on, out of the water and over a bucket, into which it was shaken loose. This method was successful at least fifty percent of the time.

Other sorties into Grassy Lake was for the purpose of turtle hunting, especially after young new hatches. We would wade along the edges in about six to twelve inches of water, and flush the baby turtles out from under the cattail reeds and debris lying on the bottom.

They would scamper out ahead of us and we could just reach down and pick them up with our hands. They were common water species; dark green with red and yellow stripes along their head, neck and legs.

I can still remember the pleasant feel of those frisky little creatures, about the size of a quarter, running over my hands and arms with their cool little webbed feet and smooth underbellies.

Chapter VII

The Barnstormers

During the summer of 1937, we were treated to an exciting event. The barnstormers were coming to Wanda Airport to put on an air show. Even today, with air travel and airplanes such an integral part of our daily lives, an air show will still draw large crowds. One can imagine the novelty and excitement such an event would create during that period. This was especially so for young impressionable boys with dreams of becoming aviators.

By 1937, airplanes had advanced considerably since World War One. However, many of the airplanes still flying were of that vintage. Keep in mind that Lucky Lindy had made his historical solo flight of the Atlantic only ten years earlier.

One piece of wearing apparel that was a testimony to the influence of aviation upon a nation of young boys, was the leather aviator cap with goggles and chin strap. In the 1930s and 40s, these were worn during the winter months more often than the standard stocking cap.

There were some drawbacks to wearing the goggles however, especially when the temperature was extremely cold accompanied by strong winds. Under these conditions, which should have been ideal, they could actually become a handicap, especially if the fit was bad. The rubber padding around the eyepiece became very hard and cold and would cause the forehead to ache. The sharp wind funneling around the sides of a loose fitting eyepiece usually caused tearing. It was more comfortable under these conditions to snap the goggles back into position on the top of the cap.

I can remember vividly the day Marvin, Tommy and I piled in Uncle Tom's Model-A and headed toward Wanda and the big show. The closer we came the more we started rubber-necking, crawling from window to window, in search of any airplanes that may be flying in the area. We didn't want to miss one exciting sight.

Shortly after we had arrived and edged up as close as we dared to where the airplanes were parked, a Curtis Robin landed and came taxiing across the ground, with its engine sputtering and choking on puffs of smoke trailing behind. It appeared to be protesting the degrading treatment of being earthbound.

We stared, no doubt with mouths agape, in reverent silence as the tall pilot, wearing knee high boots, saddle pants, and a leather jacket, uncoiled from the cockpit. We watched his every move as if he were an alien as he casually gave his airplane a walk-around inspection.

By today's standards, the sparse display of airplanes would not create much excitement, but to us each one was a magical thing. I remember easing up and putting my hand to the wing strut of one of these mysterious things. I stood awed by the thought that just a short time earlier it had been flying among the clouds, thousands of feet above the earth. Looking inside I could see the many instruments that had to be mastered by the superman that flew this machine.

The star of the air show was a Ford Tri-Motor, parked rather close to the spectator area. This was for the purpose of easy access for those paying for rides. Uncle Tom gave Tommy the three dollars that would purchase a ride lasting approximately fifteen minutes.

Marvin and I of course didn't have three dollars, and we knew Uncle Tom couldn't afford to pay for all three of us. That by no means diminished our excitement at the possibility of one of us riding in an airplane.

As Tommy lined up with other passengers preparing to board, Marvin and I were beside ourselves with excitement. I was laughing and jumping up and down as it became Tommy's turn to climb aboard. The passengers were soon settled in and we were able to see Tommy's head peeking out the window as the three big radial engines coughed and came to life.

We didn't take our eyes off the airplane as it lumbered down to the end of the grassy runway and turned into position to take off. It hesitated only for a second or two before the engines came up to full throttle. With smoke bellowing out behind, it started moving forward as if in slow motion. It gradually picked up speed and the tail wheel lifted off the ground just as it passed in front of where we were standing. Tommy could not have been more excited at that moment than Marvin and I. Just knowing that he was in that airplane was enough.

The plane broke ground and continued to slowly gain altitude in a flat climb, as if a giant invisible string was lifting it. After gaining about two hundred feet of altitude, it made a slow turn westward and continued to climb out over the Shell Refinery.

Although there were many exciting things going on around us, we couldn't keep from craning our necks to try to catch a glimpse of the big bird returning. After what seemed like an eternity, we heard the big engines before we actually saw the airplane. It emerged from behind a row of Lombardy poplar trees aligning the west side of the field, and lined up for a landing to the north. Marvin, nor I, blinked an eye from the moment it came into view and parked in front of us.

Tommy was about the fourth or fifth passenger off. He came loping toward us with his arms flapping like some giant bird trying to get back in the air. By the time he reached us, we all three were jumping up and down and talking at the same time. It took some time but eventually Tommy was able to tell of the many sights and the feeling of flying. It was a feeling that Marvin and I could only imagine.

Our attention was soon diverted from Tommy's adventure to the top billing of the show. It was the parachute jumper that supposedly had a great surprise for the spectators. This, of course, did draw our attention because it was one of the main reasons we came. In all probability there was hardly a person in attendance that had ever witnessed a parachute jump.

The parachutist stood in front of the crowd as the announcer, using a megaphone, made the introductions and ballyhooed the spectacular event we were about to witness. The jumper was dressed in leather, wearing an aviator cap with goggles. As he was being helped into his parachute, that appeared to be an endless assortment of straps and buckles, I couldn't help but think he must be the bravest man in the world.

After some final tugs and pulls, it appeared all the final adjustments were complete and he was ready. He waddled toward the open cockpit biplane (double-winger, we called them) with his low-slung parachute bouncing on his hips. He nimbly stepped up on the wing and over into the front cockpit. He stood there for a few seconds, waving to the crowd as the prop was being pulled through. When the engine came to life, he settled down into his seat and the plane slowly taxied off toward the south end of the field.

The pilot did not hesitate, but applied power as he turned for takeoff. The pilot wagged the wings of the plane as he came by us just about fifty feet off the ground, then continued to gain altitude in a climbing turn around the field.

The announcer, with his megaphone, continued his ballyhoo in an attempt to whip the crowd into a state of excitement. While telling the crowd of the danger and bravery of this young daredevil, several men were working the crowd of spectators with hats held out for donations.

Needless to say, the announcer was definitely having the desired effect on me, and I'm sure Marvin and Tommy as well. I felt as if I wanted to close my eyes and not look, then when it was all over I would tell them that I did, because I knew by the way the announcer was talking that this man was about to die, and I sure didn't want to see that.

As the plane made another turn over the field, everyone just knew this would be it. By this time, my heart was pounding so hard in my ears I could hardly hear. The announcer was telling the crowd to watch for something spectacular; something more than just a parachute jump.

Then it happened. With our heads craned back, looking almost straight up, a small object came loose from the plane. It was hard to believe that what looked like a very small stick-man, was actually our brave hero that had stood in front of us just a short time earlier. Suddenly a stream of white silk appeared and then the chute blossomed with an audible pop, and appeared to explode in a cloud of white smoke. This must be the big surprise. This was the spectacular event that we were told to look for.

The white cloud of smoke or flour that had been packed in the parachute slowly drifted to the south as the parachutist continued to float earthward. His descent was so gradual at first that it appeared he was suspended. This illusion was due to his position of being almost directly overhead. It was only after he had drifted toward the center of the field and was almost on the ground, that his rate of descent could be realized. In fact, it was quite fast and he hit the ground hard and rolled, then jumped up and waved, and took several bows to the cheering and applauding crowd.

The remaining time at the Wanda Airport that day must have been anticlimactic because I have very little memory of it. It wasn't, however, the end of our excitement over watching the parachute jumper. It must have had an overwhelming effect on Tommy, because he decided that he would have to try it himself.

Tommy lived on Velma, and at that time there was a high back porch that was about six feet off the ground, and then by standing on the railing you could add another three feet or so. Tommy thought that was sufficient for his purpose.

Tommy got one of his mother's sheets, probably one of her best, and tied ropes to the corners. He then tied the ends together and looped them under his arms. I stood by excitedly and if it worked then I would try it myself. His plan was to gather the sheet up in his arms and as he jumped, throw the sheet up in the air, thus giving it plenty of time to open before he hit the ground.

Now this plan appeared perfectly sound and we could see no reason why it wouldn't work. Tommy climbed up on the railing while I steadied him and got ready to jump. It was then that I noticed he may have had second thoughts, because there was some hesitation, but Tommy was not one to chicken out. He hesitated only another second or two, then, off he went.

Now we thought we had this thing figured out, but we had overlooked one very important detail. The ropes were not attached to him, only looped under his arms, so when he threw the sheet into the air, he literally threw his harness away with the parachute.

Tommy landed on the ground with a thud, his chute coming down beside him in a wad. He rolled around on the ground moaning and groaning. He had the wind knocked out of him and a sprained ankle. Needless to say, that was the end of experimentation with parachutes.

Chapter VIII

Shots!!!

While living on Melrose, in 1937, Mom became very ill and the doctor was summoned; in those days doctors still made house calls. His diagnosis was diphtheria. This, of course, meant that we were to be quarantined once again. The procedure was starting to become rather routine. Dad, of course, was kept away because he had to work and we kids had to fend for ourselves as best we could, and try to take care of Mom.

I can remember cooking some of the more simple dishes, such as macaroni, potatoes, and opening jars of canned goods. This, of course, was supervised by Mom from her sick bed. It was only years later that we were able to appreciate how sick she really was.

It was during Mom's sickness that we kids had to undergo one of the most frightening and humiliating experiences of our young lives—SHOTS!

In those days kids always associated the doctor's visit with awful tasting medicine or shots. Up to this time none of us had ever had an inoculation, but we sure heard the horrible tales about them, and considered them equivalent to the guillotine. But this time we really had nothing to fear because Mom was the one that was sick, right?

Shortly after the doctor had finished administering to Mom, he turned to us kids, all standing around the bed curiously watching everything, and said, "Now I'm going to have to give all you children a shot." WOW!, that's when all hell broke loose. Five kids scattered to every hiding place in the house they could find.

I'm not quite sure how, but with Mom's coaxing, the doctor was able to eventually round us up. He arranged us all on the same bed in a row, with our bare butts exposed. I've often wished that someone would have taken a picture of that, because it could have been a Norman Rockwell masterpiece.

I don't remember the lineup, but I do know that Jack was ahead of me. I watched the doctor out of the corner of my eye and saw him get his. I knew I was next, so I tensed my butt as hard as I could and got ready to let out my best blood-curdling scream.

I felt the doctor pinch my butt and then in a moment he moved on to the next kid. I actually never felt the needle and wondered if he had actually given me a shot. Although a great scream was wasted, I was greatly relieved that it was over.

Mom eventually regained her health and things were back to normal; as normal as could be expected with five rambunctious kids getting into one scrape after another.

*   *   *

I had gotten into my first fight at school; over what, I've never been able to remember. Marvin told me I got the best of him, but somehow it didn't help, I still had a sick feeling over it.

Marvin would probably have acquired a reputation as a firebug by this time, if it were known that he was the one responsible for setting the vacant lot on fire across from Charlie's Market. Don't forget the chicken house in Roxana.

We had just come from Charlie's Market where Marvin had purchased a box of penny matches. You see, we had a choice selection of grape vine that we were planning on smoking. At the corner of Park and Sinclair, across from the market, Marvin hunkered down in the tall grass to light up. Evidently one of the matches he discarded had some life in it, because we had only gone a short distance when we caught a whiff of the unmistakable smell of burning grass.

Looking back we could see the flames already raging across the field, whipped up by the hot summer winds. Needless to say, we were long gone by the time people started arriving to fight the flames.

From our hiding place behind the house we could observe the arrival of the fire truck. Some men were already there trying to beat the flames with burlap sacks or what other device they may have. With the help of the fire hoses from the truck, the situation was soon under control.

It must be noted here, that vacant lots burning were not unusual in the Roxana and South Roxana area during the hot summer months. A large percent of vacant lots would show the blackened scars of the fire before summer was over. I guess that's why there was little said about this particular incident.

*   *   *

The owl patch, one of our favorite playing areas was located off Cemetery Road just south of the cemetery about one-half mile. It was heavily wooded with large oak trees and about twenty acres in size.

These dark woods were full of mystery that kept us coming back time and again. We would walk through town and down Cemetery Road in the hot scorching summer sun, anxiously looking forward to the relief of the cool dark woods. I still remember the spot and the feel of sitting under that large shady oak at the edge of the woods. After the long hot walk, that cool gentle breeze on my hot sweaty face and bare skin was pure luxury.

The owl patch was not ours alone. There were other groups of boys from town that also used it as their playground. The boys we generally associated with were about seven to nine years of age, with a few older exceptions, Cherb McDonough being one. I believe he was about twelve and probably the oldest of the group.

Now please note that I do not refer to these groups as gangs. They did not fit the definition of what we refer to today as gangs. They were loose associations for the most part, formed mainly by age and social relationships. There were no elected leaders as such, just the natural surfacing of those with the best ideas at any given time, or the ability to persuade.

During one particular sortie to the owl patch, we ran across a group of four older boys from town. One of them had what we later learned was a starter pistol. Of course we were unaware of this at the time when the play started to get a little rough.

He took us captive and started marching us around like we were prisoners. I'm not sure why, but one of the boys from his group started to run away. The boy with the pistol immediately pulled the gun up and shot. The noise in the close woods was deafening. The boy, who was about twenty feet away by then, arched and grabbed his back and fell to the ground. We all froze in shocked silence, especially the boy holding the pistol.

Suddenly, after what seemed like an eternity, the boy holding the gun screamed hysterically "It's just a starter pistol! See! See!" holding up the gun and a blank cartridge. "It can't hurt anyone!" he cried in his defense.

About that time the boy on the ground, who had been lying lifeless, slowly got up and started walking around while rubbing his back. We immediately gathered around him and started inspecting his back. The only marks we could find were a few minor scratches that he could have received while falling to the ground.

There was a marked change in the boy with the gun. I guess he had suffered a real shock of what he thought he had done, because he looked a little pale and was no longer saying much. The remainder of the time spent at the owl patch that day was uneventful.

Chapter IX

Gene and Marvin Become Employed

The Shell Oil Refinery was just about three hundred feet from our house. Across the fence were huge petroleum storage tanks. This area was usually full of activity and occasionally an accident would occur. Most were fires that were extinguished without major difficulty. However, this was soon to change.

During the month of May 1938, we were alerted by the sounds of sirens in the distance, of which at first we gave little attention. It was only after the prolonged and persistent screaming that our attention was finally forced from our engrossing pastime of crawdad fishing.

Standing up on the old pier in Grassy Lake, we could see the smoke now starting to bellow up from the storage tank area just across the fence. We threw down our poles and took off running for home.

By the time we arrived at our house, orange flames were now visibly boiling inside the thick column of black smoke. It wasn't long before everyone was out in their yards watching. Most instantly knew that this was not going to be just another fire.

By evening the fire had spread to other tanks. The temperature was so hot that the tanks were melting in on themselves. Although, each tank had its own moat to contain spillage, the heat was so intense that adjacent tanks were being ignited.

As dark arrived, the fire was now a raging inferno, completely out of control. Standing in our yards, we could feel the heat on our faces, and our clothes were blowing from the wind created by the intense updraft.

By now, every piece of fire fighting equipment for miles around was desperately involved in containment. That was all they could do. It was well after midnight before they had it under control. The flames were still visible the next morning, but were no longer a source of danger.

*   *   *

1937 was also the year, at ages 8 and 9, that Marvin and I joined the ranks of the employed. Marvin I'm sure, had come up with the idea that we could make some money at hoeing watermelons. So one hot summer morning we hitched up the gallowses to our one piece bibbed overalls and headed for the melon patches out Poag Road.

At the first big farm we came to, Marvin I'm sure, because I can't picture me having the courage, went up to the house and asked if they needed help with hoeing. They must have been more desperate than we realized, because we were immediately put to work at the prevailing rate of one dollar a day.

It didn't take me long, while chopping at weeds hour after hour under the hot summer sun, to come to the conclusion that I was not quite ready for grownup labor. Besides, there were all those crawdads and turtles out in Grassy Lake just begging me to come and catch them. The owl patch was just waiting with all its dark mysteries to be investigated. But instead of all the important things I could be doing, I was in the middle of a melon patch, chopping, chopping, chopping...

The day finally ended and Marvin and I were paid our dollar for the day's labor. Although having hard currency in one's pocket does give one a feeling of worth and satisfaction, it somehow was not adding up to an even exchange, in my mind at least. After all, not only was I giving my labor, but also the forfeiture of all the fun I could have been having. Now that adds up to at least a two-dollar value.

Regardless of my reservations, we headed back to the patch the next morning. It was in the middle of the afternoon when I came to realize that the relentless sun wasn't going to quit; the tough crab grass wasn't going to quit, but I was. I did my best to hold out to the end of the day, but that was it.

After we had collected our dollar and were walking home, I told Marvin I wasn't going back. He tried to talk me into it, but I wasn't having any of it. I'd rather be sitting under a black willow tree on one of the many oases in the middle of Grassy Lake, or looking for baby catfish hatches boiling up in one of the many pools there. No, my farming days for now were definitely over.

Marvin continued to hoe alone for the next day or two, but then he too decided to call it quits. I'm sure if I had stuck it out he would have continued to work longer, but even for a nine year old, it got awfully lonesome out in the middle of a watermelon patch all by yourself.

Chapter X

The Christmas That Almost Wasn't

Christmas 1937 was one of the most memorable. Not because it was filled with fond memories or many gifts, but because that particular Christmas turned out to be one filled with anxiety and uncertainty.

Although our Christmases were never lavish, they were nevertheless, filled with the Christmas spirit. We always had a tree that Mom would pick up at the grocer's a few days before Christmas. In those days I don't recall Christmas trees being sold anywhere except at the grocery stores.

We put up and trimmed the tree as many days before Christmas as Mom would allow. When we were very young Mom always strung the lights and allowed us even as small children, to participate in hanging the ornaments.

As we grew older, the job of choosing and purchasing the tree fell to Marvin and me. I was delegated the responsibility, or more likely I assumed it, of mounting the tree on the stand and stringing the lights. Rita, now older and also very excited and enthusiastic during the Christmas season, began to assist in this procedure and her participation became part of our Christmas tradition.

Marvin, the director, would sit back and supervise the ritual until we were finished, then would take his turn and apply his specialty. His expertise was the hanging of the tinsel. Marvin was the icicle man. He would place each strand, one by one, with precision until each branch was uniformly covered. He then would stand back a few paces and with small pinches of tinsel, would artfully toss it toward a desired location on the tree. After all the tinsel had been placed on the tree to his satisfaction and his final inspection had been accomplished, the tree was officially considered trimmed.

Our Christmas gifts usually consisted of one major toy, for which we had asked Santa, and a couple of minor ones. We always hung our stockings and on Christmas morning found them filled with candy, nuts, and fruit.

The wrapped gifts under the tree before Christmas Day were the toys that we knew were from Mom and Dad and gifts we children had given to each other. Santa's gifts, our primary Christmas gifts, of course would not be delivered until Christmas Eve, and only after we were fast asleep.

Trying to hurry and go to sleep on Christmas Eve night so Santa could come was as hard for me as trying to hold back a cough; it was almost impossible. I would lie there for what seemed like hours and then suddenly it was morning. I never knew when it happened – I couldn't remember getting drowsy – but sleep would inevitably and mercifully come; that is until one Christmas Eve night when my older and much wiser brother decided it was time to dispel the Santa Claus myth.

Late one Christmas Eve night when I was about five years old and we were lying in bed (I no doubt staring out the window into the darkness listening for Santa's sleigh) Marvin blurted out, "You know, there is no Santa Claus!" He then continued to tell me that reindeer really couldn't fly and that all the toys were actually provided by Mom and Dad.

At this point in our lives, to me Marvin's word was gospel. I believed everything he said. What! No Santa Claus? Na! This was more than my young mind could accept. This time I was determined to stay awake all night if necessary to prove him wrong.

For the first and probably the only time in my young life, I was now actually trying to stay awake on Christmas Eve night and, wouldn't you know, it was about impossible.

Sometime during the wee hours of the morning while still struggling desperately to keep my eyes open, the logic of it all started to sink in. With unavoidable reality came frustration, then the anger and eventually, sleep.

Christmas morning that year, it seemed at first, was no different from others. Excited kids scampering about the tree, all in their own world doing their own thing and at the same time excitedly trying to see what toys the other kids were unwrapping or playing with.

Only hours later, after all the nervous energy had been expended, after most of the toys had been set aside, I realized something had changed. The melancholy hour, as I refer to it – that let down which always follows the excitement of Christmas morning was stronger this year than usual, and of course I knew why. My childhood fantasy was gone, the myth dispelled – there was no Santa Claus.

The reason that Christmas of 1937 was an exception to our customary happy Christmas holiday celebration was because of our father. Until now I've made only incidental mention of him. Our father, you see, was an alcoholic, bringing into the family all the undesirable effects of alcoholism. The worst result besides self-destruction and family humiliation, was his lack of dependability.

Mom would never know from one day to the next how much of his pay would be available for necessities. There were times when Dad would come home early the next morning, drunk and broke, without a penny in his pocket.

For our survival, Mom eventually started meeting Dad at the refinery gate on paydays. She knew she had to get to him before he slipped into one of the many taverns throughout the South Roxana and Wood River areas. There were times when he would slip by her or for some reason she was unable to meet him; then it became necessary for her to find someone with an automobile willing to drive her around to his usual hang outs to find him and salvage as much as she could of the pay the family depended on. When these tactics failed, there was nothing she could do but sit up and wait for him to come, hoping there would be something left for food and rent.

I should inject here that our father was never abusive to us children, even when he was drinking or falling down drunk. So many alcoholics become angry or mean when they're under the influence of alcohol. For Dad it was just the opposite; he was usually very playful and loving.

Although we were never afraid of our father, we did feel shame and humiliation when we would be outside playing with our friends and he would come staggering up the sidewalk. If we spotted him early enough, we would run inside the house and tell Mom. We would stay there and anxiously watch from the window his progress. If it hadn't been for the fact that it was our father, his three steps forward and one back, would have been comical.

Dad had been going through one of his drinking spells the last few weeks before Christmas, 1937. Mom, for whatever reason, had been unsuccessful in getting hold of his pay before most of it had been spent. What little she had been able to salvage had to go for food and other essentials. There was precious little left over for Christmas gifts. In fact there was none.

Somehow Mom was able to scratch up enough for a Christmas tree and by Christmas Eve it was trimmed and ready, but the floor beneath the tree was strikingly bare.

Christmas fell on Saturday that year, which meant that payday was on Friday, Christmas Eve. I can't remember why, but Mom was unable to meet Dad at the refinery gate this time. This meant that any hope we had of receiving any toys for Christmas depended solely upon Dad.

Families that have endured the horrors of an alcoholic parent understand only too well the anguish and disappointments created by alcoholism. We were no exception. As young as we were, we had already learned that you couldn't depend upon the word of an alcoholic. Their intentions may be good, but much too often they are incapable of delivering upon their promises.

By eight o'clock Christmas Eve Marvin and I were starting to get very worried. We knew from experience that the odds were not in our favor. Rita, I'm sure, also understood the situation to some degree, but Norma and Jack were still too young to be concerned. The glitter of the decorated tree was enough for them at this point in their lives.

After nine o'clock and Dad still had not come home, Marvin and I gave up and resigned ourselves to the fact that there would be no toys that year. We knew the stores closed early on Christmas Eve and therefore knew Dad would have had plenty of time to get home.

About ten o'clock Marvin and I, the only children still up, were finally encouraged to go to bed by Mom. My concern had turned from disappointment and self-pity, to one of explaining no toys for Christmas. How could I answer anyone who would ask "Gene, what did you get for Christmas?"

Trying to figure out the best answer to that question became a real dilemma. My first thought was to lie and name a few toys but, then how would I explain never playing with them? It would have been virtually impossible to keep my imaginary toys hidden from the neighborhood kids. We were constantly in and out of each other's house, especially on Christmas Day.

I could ignore the question I suppose, but that would only create more curiosity and more questions and eventually my friends would find out anyway.

I even thought of telling the truth. When asked what Santa had brought me, I could answer, "Nothing." But that wouldn't do. Such an abrupt and truthful answer would spark too much emotionalism and self-pity in me; I might even start crying.

Thankfully I didn't have to ponder that problem much longer because around midnight, our dog Polly announced Dad's arrival. Polly always knew when Dad was approaching the house long before we could see or hear him. She would jump up on the back of the couch, stare out of the window into the darkness, and continue barking, her legs all the while prancing excitedly up and down.

Marvin and I jumped out of bed and ran to the hallway where we were able to watch as he entered. It seemed an eternity before we heard his feet hit the steps of the front porch. We knew by his fumbling hesitation that he was drunk. When the door eventually opened and he stumbled through, we were no longer concerned with his state of sobriety, because the object of our concern became the large rumpled paper bag he carried. Marvin and I scrambled back to our bed and covered up our heads, trying to muffle our squirming and giggling excitement. We didn't know what Dad had in the sack, but we were certain it had to be toys.

I can't remember what time it was when I awoke Christmas morning, but I do remember going immediately to the Christmas tree. Sure enough, there were toys under the tree, not many, but there were toys. Dad managed to make it home with at least one toy for each child.

My toy was a wind-up gray and black metal Caterpillar tractor with rubber tracks. It could climb over books and other objects. Marvin received a metal wind-up airplane, a China Clipper. Rita and Norma received dolls and I can't remember Jack's toy.

The Christmas that almost wasn't turned out all right after all. Toys weren't plentiful, but there were enough – enough to provide an adequate answer to the question, "Gene, what did you get for Christmas?"

Chapter XI

Monty and Me

I glanced at my watch and realized I had been sitting in my car in this deserted graveled lot for better than an hour. I looked around at my surroundings once again and it was as if someone had suddenly changed slides in a projector. The scene had changed from one of nostalgic warmth to one that was cool and alien. There were no children playing and laughing, no activity in the rail yard, no people moving around, and much worse, no Grassy Lake. This was not the South Roxana from which we moved in 1938.

That summer we moved to 834 Halloran Avenue in Wood River, Illinois, which had to be my next destination. I started my car and with one last look, slowly drove from the lot and headed north.

As I drove, I backtracked my earlier route into Roxana and continued up Central Avenue until I came to Madison. There I turned left and drove one block before turning right on Ninth Street.

As I drove north the street names were becoming familiar. I drove past Ferguson, Lorena, Acton and Penning. As I approached the next street, which would be Halloran, I slowed to turn, then decided to continue on and try to find a restaurant and have breakfast.

At the corner of Ninth and Edwardsville Road I spotted a restaurant – the Pancake Ranch. I pulled around the corner into the parking lot and went inside. I knew as I walked through the door that this was my kind of place.

The interior was bright and cheery, and contained both booths and tables. I choose a booth that would afford me the best view and sat down. I was there only a few seconds before a waitress came my way holding a coffee pot and cup.

After ordering, I sat there sipping my coffee while watching the early morning activity; listening to the chatter of voices and clashing of dishes. It was the typical neighborhood café. Most of the customers appeared to be regulars and acquainted with each other.

The majority of the patrons were middle-aged or older. I looked into the faces of those appearing to be my age for signs of familiarity. I was speculating on the possibility that maybe at least one had grown up in the neighborhood and would be someone I had known and played with a half-century earlier. The longer I looked at them the more familiar they all appeared. I knew of course, that my mind was playing games with me.

While sitting there eating, I reflected on all the changes that had taken place. This wedge of land between Ninth Street and Edwardsville Road, on which the restaurant now sat, had been our playground back in 1938. This had been an empty lot where we sometimes played football, except when the sandburs were too thick.

A large oak tree had grown on this site back then. It was located about one hundred feet east of Ninth Street and in line with Halloran Avenue. During the summer that tree had been a very popular gathering place and play area.

There were many evenings when the young boys of the neighborhood would congregate on this spot and build a bonfire, one of our major forms of entertainment. We would sit around the fire and tell ghost stories or other wild tales. Sometimes we would stay there well past midnight, especially during the summer when we didn't have to go to school the next day.

I must add here, for historical purposes only, that we had a preferred method of extinguishing the fire when it was time to go home. We circled the fire and each boy (using the equipment nature had provided) did his best to be the one that doused the last ember. We usually ended up however, with more fire than extinguishers, and finished the job with sand.

I sat there after I had finished my third cup of coffee, musing over the kind of day this was to be. I was in no hurry; I had the entire day to do nothing except to drive around the area and reminisce, so I continued to sit there and listen to the banter between the customers and waitresses.

After having been there for about an hour, I finally decided it was time to move on. I paid my bill and left, considering returning later in the day for lunch or maybe dinner.

As I drove out of the parking lot and headed west on Edwardsville Road, I passed a small hamburger stand where once McCune's gas station had stood. Because Frances, Dewey, and Johnny McCune were in the same age group as Marvin and me, we had played together often and the station had been the focus of our activity.

One block west of Ninth Street, I turned left onto McHugh Street, then eased up and parked just short of the stop sign at McHugh and Halloran. From this vantage point I was looking directly at the house we had moved to in 1938 – 834 Halloran Avenue.

*   *   *

The house had changed some, but mostly for the better. The front porch that had been open when we lived there, was now closed in. The back porch, which I couldn't see from my position, I later found out it too had been closed in. The house was still white, but black shutters had been added. The one thing that impressed me most, however, was that beautiful American flag waving at the front porch.

The house appeared much closer to the sidewalk than I remembered. The front yard had shrunk. A large maple tree that had once grown there was gone, along with the ones that had lined the east side of the lot. I could see that the grape arbor at the southeast side of the back yard was gone. Many of the homes in the Wood River area had arbors in their backyards during the 1930s and 40s. They were usually the dark blue concord variety.

In 1938, this house had stood alone with open lots on either side. There was only one open lot on the east side. To the west, there were no houses until well beyond Dulaney Avenue.

From the position that my car was parked, I could see a spot at the southeast corner of the house that once had been my favorite place. The spot was sandy and I could make roads for my toy cars, or whatever object I could find to pretend was my car. The house had provided protection from the cool prevailing northwesterly winds, and the early morning sun warmed the area quickly.

While sitting in my car looking at the spot, I couldn't help but recall a morning recently when I had awakened and while still in a dreamy state, the images of this spot came to me as if it had only been yesterday.

All through that day and the next, I couldn't keep from thinking about those images. They were so clear that I felt moved to put them into verse, which I've titled "A Day of My Youth." It is included in another book that I've written – "Tales of Pigeon Roost Hollow and More."

*   *   *

HUCKLEBERRY HEART:
THE BOYS OF HALLORAN AVENUE

When Marvin and I first received the news that we were going to move, we were very upset. To leave our friends and all the adventure the South Roxana area provided us was unthinkable. Moving and making new friends proved not nearly as upsetting as we first supposed it would be.

The move from South Roxana to Halloran Avenue was only two and one-half miles away. This meant that Marvin and I could hike that distance any time the mood would strike, which it frequently did at first. Also, Tommy still lived there, which meant that we would be visiting often.

The rest of that first summer on Halloran was spent getting acquainted with the neighborhood and the kids. It turned out that there were many kids of our age group living within a one-block radius.

In addition to the three McCune boys that I've previously mentioned, there was Roland McCune, who was a few years older. The Ritters, Tootsie and Bobby, lived across the street from us at the corner of McHugh and Halloran. Jack, Benny, Donald, and Marlene Stahlheber, lived next door to the Ritters. Bob and Herb Paton lived across the street and two doors west of the Stalhebers.

The Scoggin boys lived on the corner across McHugh Street, opposite the Ritters. Artie (Arthur) and Billy Roos lived at the northeast corner of Halloran and Ninth. Bobby Moore lived at the northeast corner of Penning and Ninth; and Monty, Joyce, and Howard Heffner lived across the street, next to the last house from the corner of Halloran and Ninth Street. Roger Raines lived at the west end of Halloran Avenue, across Sixth Street in a big white house. Donald Harper, with whom I buddied around with, lived behind us over on Penning.

Many other kids that eventually became friends lived within a three-block radius, whose names I've forgotten, but nevertheless played a part in our daily activities while we lived there.

Of all the children we played with, Monty Heffner was my closest friend. Although personality wise we were opposite in many ways, we each had an adventurous spirit. Monty's personality was outgoing, demonstrative, and hyper. He always walked with a bounce. I, on the other hand, was reserved and quiet and yes, very bashful.

It was this friendship and our excursions throughout the area that prompted me some years ago to write the following verse.

GENE NELSON ISOM

Monty and Me

Two young boys not yet in our teens
Inseparable in every way,
Together in most activity,
At school as well as play.

But little did we know
Back in the nineteen thirties;
So young and eager then,
For life's many mysteries.

With my Daisy Red Rider,
We would go forth each day
And with Monty's too
Oh what quarry we would slay.

Between houses and alleyways
We'd slip and stalk,
From garage to garbage can
In but a whisper we'd talk.

Between Halloran and Penning
And Acton too,
We sleuthed with cunning
For all predators in view.

Sparrows were pugnacious birds,
Much larger than a hen.
Starlings were of a species
That would prey upon men.

Rodents were tigers
As fierce as could be,
But they were no match for
Ol' Daisy, Monty and me.

* * *

HUCKLEBERRY HEART:
THE BOYS OF HALLORAN AVENUE

Between Dulaney and Prospect
And Edwardsville Road,
The carnivorous Meadow Lark
In fields did abode.

We slithered on our bellies
For what seemed like an hour,
Between sage clump and sandbur
For one shot that went sour.

Through Fox's Grove we'd often trek,
By chance to spot Reynard;
But better had we known,
We were in his own back yard.

Through the oak and sycamore
And between the tidy ash,
We'd rarely glimpse the wisp
As he made his wildly dash.

Though we sought to persevere
To fulfill our considered decree;
It was a hardy task indeed, for
Ol' Daisy, Monty, and me.

*   *   *

We'd hike to the top of the mountain,
Toward the end of Ninth Street,
To view the vexing squirrels,
Frolicking among the bittersweet.

We'd sally forth to Berry's woods,
Then end up at Boman's pond:
From sun up to sun down,
We secured the area far and yond.

Throughout Spring, Summer, and Fall,
We were always on patrol;
Through Vaughn's woods and Indian Creek
For vicious varmints to control.

Even amid blustering winter,
With our right hand mitten cut free,
To loose the ready trigger finger,
For quick action, can't you see?

I'm sure we were recognized,
But of course not by all,
As the two young knights of Halloran,
Responding to duty's call.

There was no need to worry,
They could sleep fast you see;
For the realm was well protected, by
Ol' Daisy, Monty, and me.

Chapter XII

The Young Izaak Walton

The years that we lived in Wood River were probably the most enjoyable and adventurous of all my formative years. Although I became aware of the nature and the animal world while living in South Roxana, it was on Halloran Avenue that I truly became aware of the world around me. It was here in this Midwestern setting that I grew into young adulthood.

We'd only been living on Halloran a couple of days when we became acquainted with the Stalheber boys, the first that we started playing with regularly. It was they who introduced us to the term "hiking." Instead of saying "Let's go," we now were saying, "Let's hike," when one of us suggested going someplace.

During the next few years, there was not one spot within the metropolitan area that we didn't hike to. Some of our daily hikes would extend as far as the Piasa Bird, painted on the bluff west of Alton, and to the east as far as Edwardsville; north to Bethalto, and south as far as the Cahokia Diversion Channel below South Roxana. These daily hikes ranged in distance from one to eight miles.

One of the first hikes on which Marvin and I accompanied Jack, Benny and Don Stalheber was to the Ninth Street hill woods. That area remained one of our favorites and over the years we would spend many long days there.

The spot where we spent most of our time is now a cul-de-sac at the end of Forest Drive. That area was the highest point on the hill and all of Wood River could be viewed from there, that is, whenever you could find an opening to see through the foliage. Large trees grew there, along with wild grape vines and thick brush.

It was those grape vines that held the biggest attraction. One had been cut and trimmed into a swing. We would pull it back as far up the hill as possible,

65

then swing out over the slope to about thirty feet above the ground. Sometimes, taking water and a lunch, we would roam those woods from early morning to late evening.

Another vine that grew at that spot along with the wild grape was the bittersweet. In the fall we would climb the trees and harvest as many clumps of the small orange and red ornamental blossoms as we could.

Gathering bittersweet was no easy task. Sometimes we would work for hours only to harvest enough to make ten or fifteen small bundles, which we would peddle throughout the neighborhood for five cents each. We were usually successful in selling about half. The remaining bundles would be given to our mothers. Mom would put hers in a small vase and place it on the sideboard or on some other piece of furniture in the dining room.

The little red berry in the center of the opened orange hull would shrivel with time, but would retain its color. The small bouquets would remain attractive throughout the winter. It was usually well up into spring before Mom would throw them out. To this day, bittersweet has remained a favorite with me. I still collect it whenever I have the opportunity.

I suppose the reason we would spend so much time at Ninth Street hill woods was because of its closeness. It was located about a mile north of Halloran Avenue and we could walk there in just a few minutes.

There were a few houses along Ninth Street north of Edwardsville Road. They were located on the west side as you crossed over Edwardsville Road. Once past these houses, there was nothing between us and the top of the hill, except for the narrow asphalt road. Everything to the east of Ninth Street was farmland, and on the west side, nothing but the airport and swamp.

During the hot summer days, the tar on the road would become soft, and in some spots actually melt into small puddles of hot tar. As we hiked up the road barefooted, we did our best to hop over or walk around these hot spots. We would walk at the edge of the road as much as possible, but there were times when the sandburs were so thick we would have to stay in the road.

By late summer, after the soles of our feet had become as tough as shoe leather, these blacktopped roads gave us less concern.

There were other attractions that would cause us to hike up Ninth Street. One was the riding stables located there. When Monty Heffner and I were about eleven years old, we would work around the stables in exchange for the privilege of riding the horses.

We would spend what seemed to be hours scooping out the stalls, just for one ride that lasted about twenty or thirty minutes.

The riding trail started at the stables area and crossed over Ninth Street and then wound through the woods on the west side of the road, then circled back across the road to the stable.

After the ride I always knew I had been gypped, but that didn't deter me. Within a few days Monty and I would be back, scooping again.

Another attraction that kept us hiking up Ninth Street was Boman's Pond. Quite often however, we would approach the pond from the south end. This was true in the hot summer, because it was cooler, and besides, we would much rather be in the woods. This meant walking up the ravine to the spillway located at the south end of the pond.

Boman's Pond had been one of the major swimming holes in the Wood River area until 1926. This ended with the completion of the Wood River swimming pool. However, in 1938, it was still a favorite spot, especially for young boys who liked to fish.

We fished mostly with cane poles and sometime throw lines. It was a rare occasion when someone was seen fishing with a casting rod and reel. That's why I was so proud when I received one for my ninth birthday.

I had been looking at the rods and reels every time I walked into Ben Franklin's downtown on Ferguson Avenue. They were in a barrel to the left of the door as you entered. The rods and reels were actually sold separately – twenty-five cents each.

My birthday, September 5th, coming about the time school started was always a sore spot with me. I considered it a dirty trick to have your birthday so close to an event I dreaded worse than getting a tooth pulled. One year school actually started on my birthday.

I had mentioned to Mom a few days earlier that I would like to have a rod and reel for my birthday and she said, "I'll see what I can do."

On the morning of my birthday Mom gave me the fifty cents; two quarters. I can't remember a problem with tax. If there had been, it would have been somewhere in the neighborhood of one or two mils. I can remember Mom having to use these small button size coins when tax was required for the purchase of certain items. One mil, equivalent to one tenth of a penny, surely would not go far in today's economy.

I went to school that morning taking the money with me. It was my intention to go directly to Ben Franklin's as soon as school let out. Every few minutes throughout the day I would reach into my pocket and check on my money. While moving around, I would reach down and shake my pocket just to hear the quarters rattle.

The teacher that day may as well have been talking to the wall as far as I was concerned. She didn't know it, but I had been there in body only. My head had spent the entire day at Boman's Pond, catching thousands of catfish and sun perch.

As soon as the school bell rang, I ran out the door and headed straight to Ben Franklin's. After I purchased my rod and reel, the clerk asked if I needed some hooks and line to go with it. I said, "Na, I've got all that stuff at home." The truth was I intended to use the hooks and sinker from my cane pole. I didn't know where I would get the line.

As soon as I arrived home I started gathering up all the fishing tackle I could find. I went to the garage and stripped the couple of cane poles that were there. I scrambled the contents of the bedroom closet, if that were possible, searching every corner and crevice for something to use for line.

While searching the kitchen pantry, I came across a ball of kite string – heavily used, of course, but it would have to do.

Bt the time I finally had my rod and reel rigged and ready for use, it was almost dark. I ran outside and in the driveway along side the house, I started practicing. My first cast was a disaster. The line shot out about ten feet with a loud zing and caught, resulting in a terribly tangled backlash.

The results were the same for the first few casts, each time requiring about five minutes to untangle the line. By the time I figured out that the small elongated sinker from my cane pole was not heavy enough, it was completely dark. The next evening after school, I was at it again. I had found an old hexagon nut that weighed about one ounce and had tied that on the end of my line, hoping this would be enough weight to pull the line out and prevent backlash.

The first cast with the additional weight proved me wrong. The line shot out, the reel backlashed, and the line parted. The nut and about twenty feet on my line sailed through the air and hit the garage door with a bang.

This was not turning out the way I had planned. I was starting to become a little frustrated. My dreams of becoming known as the local Isaak Walton were fast fading.

I continued to practice and work at it however, and by dark had figured out that I could reduce the frequencies and severity of the backlashes by applying thump pressure to the reel while casting. This reduced the distance of my casts considerably, but it was a tradeoff that I was willing to accept.

By Friday night I was all set. I had spent that evening after school making my final preparations for the big day. I made my fish stringer, extra long just in case, from a piece of cord with a six-inch long stick approximately one-quarter inch in diameter, tied to each end. I then gathered all the fishing tackle I had been able to scrounge up and placed it all in a small brown paper bag.

Finding fishing worms in early September was not an easy task. The weather was still hot and the ground very dry. I finally found about two dozen, most in a spot beneath the grape arbor, after I had dug up most of the backyard. I figured this would do me for starters and if I needed more bait, I would catch grasshoppers along the bank of the pond.

It was my intention to get up around daylight Saturday morning and leave the house before anyone else was up. When I opened my eyes the next morning, bright sunlight was coming through the window and I could hear Mom stirring in the kitchen. I lay there for a moment or two before realizing where I had intended to be by this time of the morning.

I jumped out of bed, jerked on my overall pants and shirt, and headed toward the back door. As you may have noted, the uniform of the day had now changed. Marvin nor I would no longer be caught dead in bibbed overalls. The pants were the same except for the gallowses.

As I passed Mom working in the kitchen, she asked, "Where are you going in such a hurry?" "Fishing," I replied as I started out the door. "Whoa!" Mom yelled, "Not until you have eaten breakfast."

I hurriedly ate whatever Mom had forced on me and finally got underway. I grabbed my fishing tackle and worms, strategically stashed at the corner of the back porch the night before, for a silent early morning getaway.

As I hiked up Ninth Street, the early morning sun was already getting hot. I took the ravine route because I wanted to approach the pond as inconspicuously as possible. I didn't want the other fishermen that might already be there to be overly concerned with their competition. There was no one near the spillway as I walked up the levy and came into full view of the pond. There were approximately ten people there already fishing, but most were located along the east side of the pond. I had the entire spillway area to myself.

In my nervousness to make my first cast I could hardly bait the hook, but finally the big moment. I wound up and let go with a loud screeching cast. "Ugh," every head on the pond turned in my direction and stared directly at me. For some reason that I didn't fully understand, I felt embarrassingly conspicuous; but not for long.

Normally, when we fished with cane poles, we would prop them up on a forked stick or stick the end of the pole in the ground, then sit back and wait.

But not with this rig; this was a hands-on operation. I just knew the action was going to be too hot and heavy to put the rig down.

I stood there rigidly nervous, watching the tip of my rod for the slightest movement. After a minute or two and no action, I just knew that something must be wrong. I must have thrown my bait off with my cast. Yes, that had to be it, so I reeled my line in and checked it. No, that wasn't it; the worm was still there. Thinking that maybe I needed more bait, I added a second worm and cast out the second time. My cast this time was silent because I remembered to turn the "clicker" off.

While standing there, again staring at the end of my rod, my attention was drawn to some excited activity across the pond. One of the kids was pulling in a fish. The noise created by the fish flopping on the surface of the water was magnified in the quiet calm of the early morning. Although I felt a little envy, it did peak my excitement somewhat.

After having been at it for the better part of an hour, and having made dozens of casts to every part of the pond I could reach, I was becoming very discouraged.

My pole was now leaning in the fork of a stick. I had decided a few minutes earlier that the hands-on requirement was not really necessary after all. It was just too much work.

I had been sitting on the ground, Indian fashion for about ten minutes, thoroughly discouraged, when it happened. I caught a movement out of the corner of my eye. I jerked my attention back to my rod and stared at the tip. After a few seconds, I was beginning to believe that I had just imagined that my rod tip had moved, when it jerked again. I jumped forward, grabbing my rod, and gave a mighty heave backward. I lost my balance but quickly recovered and started reeling. Sure enough, I had a fish.

As I continued to reel, the fish broke the surface about ten feet from the bank. As it splashed on the surface, I took a quick glance around to assure myself that everyone around the pond was watching. With the knowledge that they were, I finished landing my trophy with a deliberate calm and skill of a professional.

After I had pulled the fish upon the bank, I picked it up by the string and held it out to one side, making sure that everyone could see. I held my rod and reel up with the other hand and posed, pretending that I was only making a thorough inspection of my catch. It was a dandy eight-inch yellow bullhead catfish.

With my enthusiasm regained, I was now prepared to spend the whole day. By the time I called it quits, I had managed to catch two more, both slightly smaller than the first. Holding all three up on the stringer together, they appeared much larger.

On the hike back home, holding the fish at my side with my rod and reel over my shoulder, I was truly the proud fisherman. It is strange how so little can become so much after expectations had been so much higher.

Chapter XIII

Just a Little Slip

Three of us children were now in school. Rita and I were attending Washington School and Marvin attended the Wood River School. These two schools, along with the Lewis-Clark School, were all located on the site where the Lewis-Clark Middle School is now located.

The three schools were in proximity to each other on one long block facing Lorena Avenue, between Fourth and Sixth Streets. Washington was next to Sixth Street, Lewis-Clark in the middle, with the Wood River School on the west end near Fourth Street.

Grades one through eight were divided up between the three schools. If my memory hasn't failed me, Washington housed grades first through third, Wood River School, fourth through sixth, and Lewis-Clark, seventh and eighth.

These schools were only four or five blocks from where we lived on Halloran, depending upon which we were attending.

That first school year in Wood River dragged by with few memorable events. I can remember, however, that the seat that I chose for my self on the first day of school was next to the last, located in the middle of the room. Monty Heffner took the last seat directly behind me.

For the next couple of years this started out as our normal seating arrangement. However, after about six or eight weeks the teacher would feel there was a need to separate us. Invariably I was the one that always had to move to the front. I wasn't able to figure out if the teacher was separating me from Monty, or Monty from me.

Monty and I were never mischievous in school; at least not most of the time. I think because we had so many interests in common, outside the classroom, that we were probably whispering too often planning our next sortie.

The few events that I do remember that first year were the Pledge of Allegiance to the Flag each morning, The Maypole Dance, and one other assignment that I've never forgotten; a homework assignment to write a poem.

Homework was something that I never did like or understand. My philosophy was, "School is school, home is home, and the twain shall never meet." So, with this in mind, it's understandable that I would arrive at school the next morning without a poem.

While sitting at my desk shortly after the school bell had rung, I suddenly got that sick feeling in the pit of my stomach. I just knew that the first thing the teacher would ask as soon as the Pledge of Allegiance was over was, "Do you all have your homework?" I also knew I'd probably be the first one she would call upon.

Taking advantage of what little time I had, I desperately started grasping for ideas, looking around the room for anything that I could write about. The more desperate I became, the less my mind would function.

Sure enough, it was the first subject that the teacher wanted to cover that morning. Luckily, I was not the first to be called upon, but I knew that what little time I had was fading. While one of the other boys was reciting his poem, I just happened to look out the window and see that it was still raining, and I knew I had to write a poem about rain.

I scribbled as fast as I could while a couple more kids went through the agony of recital. I began to have a little more confidence. After what I'd heard so far, I knew I couldn't do much worse.

Finally the moment of truth came and it was my turn. When the teacher called my name I was petrified with stage fright, but somehow I was able to stand alone while every kid in the class stared directly at me. I had hastily read what I had written only a few moments before. I've never forgotten those three little lines. "The rain is raining on the ground. The rain is raining on the fields and town. The rain is raining all around." I'd hardly gotten the last word out before I was back in my seat.

The teacher gave me a contemplating look. I didn't know if it was one of amazement, astonishment, or disgust, but she finally said in a monotone voice, "Gene, that was good!"

It really didn't matter what she thought about my first attempt at poetry. What grade she would assign my first artistic endeavor at the moment was of no importance. What was important was that it was over. Now I could sit back and watch the agony of those remaining.

There was one other incident that occurred while in that classroom that I've also never forgotten. It's one of those normal bodily functions that no one will ever admit to, but finds very amusing when someone else makes a little…slip-up.

It was during one of the quiet moments in the room when everyone was engrossed in their own study, that a very slight, but yet unmistakable sound was heard.

At first all heads remained down. A slight giggle was then heard, and then another. I turned around and pointed at Monty. He shook his head and pointed back at me. Knowing it wasn't me, I shook my head and pointed back at him. By now most of the kids in the room could no longer hold back and were laughing out loud. The teacher caused an abrupt silence with a stern "All right, that's enough!"

There was total silence except for one boy that must have thought it awfully funny, because he could remain silent only momentarily, then he would bust out again. The teacher's scolding would silence him only for about thirty seconds before he would bust loose. Each time he would snicker, the rest of the class would also start. The teacher finally had to send him from the room and have him sit in the hallway until the giggling urges passed.

Chapter XIV

Learning to Swim

In 1939, the war in Europe was expanding rapidly. Germany had invaded Poland. Great Britain, France and South Africa had declared war on Germany, and Russia had invaded Finland.

The German battleship "Graf Spee," was sunk off the coast of Uruguay and they lost their heavy cruiser, "Nurnburg," to British submarines.

Prosperity seemed just around the corner in 1939. This was due to the orders of military supplies and equipment flooding the nation's factories.

Here at home President Roosevelt had ordered all ports closed to submarines of nations that were called belligerent nations. He also signed a Neutrality Act – allowing the U.S. to aid European allies, England and France.

"You Can't Take It With You," won the Academy Award for the best picture for 1939. The Pulitzer Prize winning novel that year was "The Yearling," By Marjorie Rawlings. Another very popular novel was "The Grapes of Wrath," by John Steinbeck.

This was the start of the big band era. The more famous names were Harry James, Les Brown, Tommy Dorsey and Woody Herman. The famous Glenn Miller band would come along a few years later.

The songs that were being played that year were: "Day In – Day Out," "You Go To My Head," "South Of The Border," "Amapola," "Undecided Now," "I Can Dream Can't I."

Other newsworthy events were: King George VI became the first British monarch to visit the U.S.; Lou Gehrig's record of consecutive games played ended at 2,130; and Pan American Airways began the first regular Trans-Atlantic air service with its new airplane, the "Dixie Clipper." And on Halloran Avenue I was singing "Happy Days Are Here Again" – school was out. "School's out, school's out, the teacher let the mules out." Yes, that was a tune we could skip home to.

School was out and summer was almost here. To me this meant freedom—the freedom to fill each day with whatever exciting activity I chose. I was free to fish, to hunt, to take long daily hikes to wherever the day's adventure was expected to be and most of all, to swim.

Swimming was the special thing we did that summer, more than any other. From the first day the Wood River pool opened in the summer and until it closed in the fall, we were there. Even on days that we fished or hiked, we usually had gone to the pool earlier, or we would go later.

The summer before, after moving to Wood River, we would go to the pool whenever we could scrape up the ten or fifteen cents admission fee. We had arrived too late in the summer to purchase season tickets, which cost three dollars.

The Wood River swimming pool was financed by the Standard Oil Company and completed in 1926. It was a three hundred by two hundred foot oval and reportedly the largest in the United States.

The Grand Opening occurred on July 4, 1926, with over fifteen thousand people in attendance. The day before, the City of Wood River conducted a huge parade with many floats and Model-T ford cars decorated for the occasion.

The parade concluded at what had previously been known as Central Park, but now had been renamed Recreational Park. At the conclusion of the parade, the American Legion conducted a flag-raising ceremony.

The entire park included the pool, a round house for dancing, and wooden bandshell, was a gift from the Standard Oil Company. The company continued to totally finance the park until 1958.

When first opened, the pool was so popular that the length of time bathers could spend in the pool had to be timed so others waiting to use the pool could do so. After the pool had been open for a while rationing was dropped, but I can remember many hot summer days when it was very crowded. This usually happened on Saturdays during the middle of summer. There were times when it was virtually impossible to find an open spot to sit or lie down on the wide concrete apron that encircled the pool.

The depth of the water was about one foot at the outer edge, gradually deepening to approximately eleven feet below the diving platform located slightly south of center.

Lighting for the pool was provided by a circle of lights located on columns out in the water about twenty feet from the edge. A series of chains were attached between each column and served as a safety barrier.

The lifeguards made sure that young children or those who couldn't swim remained outside these chains. When the pool was full, the two lifeguards remained standing on their platforms, continually blowing their whistles at someone for violating the rules.

The first summer, most of my swimming consisted of thrashing the water between the edge and the chains. It was here that I slowly built my confidence and became comfortable with my head under water. Eventually I was able to swim from the shallow water to the chains with my head under water, but was still having trouble swimming any distance on the surface.

Located beyond the chains about half way toward the center of the pool were two platforms approximately one hundred feet apart. These platforms, called plunge boards, were only a few inches above the surface of the water.

A few of the boys that I knew, who were a little older and better swimmers, would spend a lot of time out on the boards, while I was left to play in the shallows by myself. My goal was to hurry and learn to swim well enough to join them.

With practice comes accomplishment, and eventually I was swimming parallel to the chain, the distance from one light post to another, without my feet touching the bottom.

I would stand at the chain as near one of the plunge boards as I could, trying to get up enough courage to swim to it. I knew it was not far, because I had been swimming a much farther distance in the shallows. It was the deep water that caused my hesitation.

Finally I was determined I was going to do it. I made up my mind that the only way to get there was to start swimming. I picked a moment when no one was watching and no other swimmers would likely come between the plunge board and me. With heart pounding, I braced my feet against the light column, took a deep breath and pushed off.

I probably looked like a side-wheeler steamboat, with both arms flailing so fast. I knew I was expending ten times the energy needed, but I also knew I couldn't stop before I got there.

I looked up just as one arm slapped down on the edge of the board. I grabbed hold and held on tight with both hands and looked around for a moment or so, then pulled myself up on the platform and just sat there.

The proud feeling didn't last long before I started becoming concerned about getting back. I felt very apprehensive and insecure sitting there while other kids were playfully running and pushing each other.

Getting back to safe water was fast becoming my major concern and also my biggest fear. Sitting there, I realized that I had never started swimming while treading in deep water, or after jumping into deep water. The only way I had ever started on my forward motion was by pushing off from the bottom with one foot.

Almost near panic, I got up and walked to the far end of the board and when the way was clear, I ran and leaped out into the water as far as I could, then continued to swim under water, froglike, until I had to surface for air. After I surfaced, I thrashed the last few feet to the chain, grabbed hold and stood up.

There was no holding back after that first swim beyond the barrier. Within a few days I was spending most of my time at the plunge boards. It was only a week or so later that I accomplished my last big hurdle – I was standing at the very top of the diving platform in the middle of the pool, the feeling and view were terrific.

My cousin Tommy told me that his first dive from the diving platform resulted in a belly flop and he never tried to dive from there again.

Chapter XV

Interrupted Summer

By the middle of the summer of 1939, I was enjoying my unrestricted daily activity to the fullest. I had learned to swim with a degree of proficiency and was trying to build up my courage to start diving from the low board of the diving platform, when my swimming for the summer ended.

One morning I awoke with a stomach ache. I had been planning to go swimming that morning and probably would have if Mom would have let me, but she insisted I just hang around the house for the day and take it easy. Although I may have protested some, it was with little enthusiasm. By the next morning I was really sick and remained in bed all day. It was toward evening while Mom was helping me to the bathroom that she realized how sick I really was. As soon as I got inside, I lay down on the cool linoleum covered floor and said, "Mom, just let me stay here." It was then that Mom really became frightened and ran to the neighbor's house to call the doctor.

When Dr. Robinson arrived he made a quick examination and said, "We've got to get this boy to the hospital immediately." It was evident to him that I was showing symptoms of acute appendicitis.

Mom also had called Aunt Wave who had arrived a while before the ambulance. Dr. Robinson had already left for the hospital to prepare for my arrival.

While Mom and Aunt Wave were fussing around my bed and praying, I remember remarking, "Why did this have to happen to me?" Aunt Wave replied, "You didn't want this to happen to some other little boy, did you?" If it really had to happen to someone, I wanted to blurt out, "Yes!" but I knew the answer I was expected to give, so in a weak and pitiful voice, answered, "No."

The ambulance arrived within a very short time and I was placed on the stretcher. As I was being wheeled out the door, Marvin, Rita, Norma, and Jack were standing there staring in wide-eyed shock.

After they had placed me in the ambulance, Mom got in with me. Aunt Wave was going to stay and watch the other kids until Mom could get back home. Dad was working the late shift at the refinery and wouldn't be home until after midnight.

As the ambulance drove toward St. Joseph Hospital in Alton, I remember asking Mom as we crossed the Wood River Bridge, why they were not using their siren. Although very sick and feverish, I was disappointed that the siren wasn't on.

Within one hour of my arrival at the hospital, I was in surgery. I awoke early the next morning, extremely sick. It was several days before I was aware of much of the activity around me.

Later I was told that my appendix had ruptured and the infection had spread throughout my lower abdomen. The surgery was very lengthy and in order to allow the infection to drain, two large rubber tubes were left protruding from my abdomen.

It was six weeks before I was allowed to leave the hospital. The first half of my stay passed rather quickly because I was unaware of so much of it. It was the last three weeks that caused me so much grief.

I was now well enough to realize that I was missing so much fun. All my friends were either swimming or hiking in the woods. I knew Monty was probably out there somewhere with his BB gun hunting in Vaughn's Woods and creek. Marvin, Benny, and Don Stahlheber were probably at the swimming pool, and I was bored stiff.

Nurse Black had taught me how to make a chain stitch with the window curtain cord at the side of my bed. I would sit there and chain stitch the cord over and over again. After I had stitched it as high as I could reach, I would rip it out with one long pull.

The worst times were when I knew that a particular activity was taking place, such as our church picnic. It was being held, as it was every year, at the Lewis and Clark Park, located on the bank of the Mississippi River. The spot was designated as the location of Lewis and Clark's campsite prior to exploration of the Louisiana Purchase in 1804.

From my window I could look south down the river toward the location. I could visualize all the things Marvin, Tommy, and the other kids were doing, while I just lay there feeling sorry for myself.

At last the big day came – I was going home. Although I had been released from the hospital, my activity was extremely limited. Not only because my ordeal had left me so weak, but also because of my infection, the tubes protruding from my stomach were left in place for additional drainage.

For the first few days at home, I remained in bed. Eventually I was allowed to slowly move around inside the house and after a week or so, to venture outside.

During my second visit to Dr. Robinson's office on Ferguson Avenue, he decided to remove the drainage tubes. The removal only caused a slight nauseous feeling.

After the removal of the tubes, a hole the size of a quarter remained open on the right side of my abdomen. The nurse dressed it with a fresh bandage and I was released. The doctor warned Mom that I was to do no lifting or straining until the opening had healed over sufficiently, which took about four weeks. What neither of them knew was that I had hiked to Ninth Street Hill woods and swung on the grape vine a few days earlier.

About one week after the doctor released me, Mom happened to look out the kitchen window and caught me playing baseball in the field next to the house. Needless to say, I made sure I was out of sight from then on.

Because of the hole in my abdomen, I was unable to go swimming for the remainder of that summer vacation, but it was impossible for me to remain inactive. I spent the rest of the summer with Monty, roaming Vaughn's Woods and Creek with our trusty BB guns.

The swamp was another area where we spent a lot of our time. The swamp was located at the foot of the hill below the cemetery, between Sixth and Ninth Streets.

This area provided Monty and me with many hours of exciting activity. The swamp was filled with cattails and sage grass, with pockets of water holes, vast areas of wet marshy ground, and patches of Black Willow thickets. In many ways, the swamp was a microcosm of Little Grassy Lake in South Roxana.

Although there were a variety of snakes in the swamp, our quarry was most often the poisonous cottonmouth. Whenever we would bag one of those babies, we considered ourselves on the same level as the famous Frank Buck. Of course Frank Buck supposedly always brought them back alive. We had no such intention.

We had no problem in identifying the cottonmouth from harmless water snakes. Whenever we came upon a snake of any kind, we would first try to examine the head to see if it had the shape of the pit viper. If for any reason that was not possible, we would try to agitate it into rearing back and widely display the pure white satin lining on the inside of the snake's mouth, from which its name derives.

During the next few years we explored the swamp area often. The swamp also was where I killed my first rabbit some years later, while hunting with a twenty-gauge shotgun that our father had bought for Marvin and me.

About the same time that I had fully recovered from my surgery and was back in shape to fully take advantage of what was left of summer, school started and I celebrated my tenth birthday.

The start of school that year was different than the previous because our sister Norma was starting the first grade at Washington School. Norma's attending school made a big difference in Marvin's and my life. Our daily routine changed considerably, since the effects of Norma having had polio meant she was unable to walk to school.

Norma had been fitted for braces on both legs at Barnes Children's Hospital in St. Louis, Missouri. On the right leg the brace came all the way to her hip and on the left leg, only as far as the knee. Although Norma could get around surprisingly well with her braces and crutches, she could not walk long distances. It therefore became her older brothers responsibility to push her to and from school in a wheelchair.

Marvin, being the older and more mature, did a better job at performing this responsibility than I. Because of all the after school activity, I usually arranged with Marvin to allow me to push her to school and he would see that she got home.

Because of the wheelchair, we had to leave for school a little earlier than previously, because we had to stay on the sidewalks and could not take our customary short cuts through the vacant lots.

Pushing a wheelchair on the sidewalks during that time was not always easy. The sidewalks were not always in the best condition. They were riddled with large cracks and frost heaves at the joints, which had to be navigated over or around.

Marvin and I accepted this responsibility naturally and never felt imposed upon. However, I must admit, ashamedly so, that several times when I was supposed to push Norma home after school, I'd almost get home, or to some other activity before I realized that I had forgotten her. I would run as hard as I could all the way back to school without stopping, and find her sitting patiently in her wheelchair outside the school door, all alone. Even today when I think about those times I'm still ashamed of myself and get a little teary-eyed. Because of our current litigious nature, I would hate to think what a school district of today would be liable for under the same circumstances.

Chapter XVI

Halloween Pranks

Autumn was always an exciting time of year. It wasn't long after school started that the air began to contain an early morning nip. Soon we would awaken to find that Ol' Jack Frost had made a visit during the night.

With the turning of the leaves of hard maple, ash, and oaks into a profusion of colors and the sweet pungent smell of dried burning leaves drifting over the town, we knew that Halloween was just around the corner.

Displays of corn stalks, pumpkins, and multicolored gourds along side of witches would start appearing on porches and in yards. Twisted black and orange crepe paper could soon be seen adorning most schoolrooms, along with a multitude of childish crayon-drawn Halloween pictures pasted on the hallway walls.

With the arrival of Halloween came thoughts of "Tricking or Treating," but, the boys of Halloran were more excited about thoughts of tricking than receiving treats.

All the kids in our neighborhood would make trips to the cornfields, mostly Berry, Reilley or Vaughn's, and pick up the nubbins of corn ears left behind after the picking. No matter how well the field had been harvested, there was always enough to be found to serve our purposes.

Often we would be returning from one of our hikes to Indian Creek, or some other favorite spot during this time of year and while walking through the harvested fields, we would pick up any ears we could find. At times, I would arrive home with corn sticking out of every pocket and my arms full.

We would shell the corn into a bag, usually a small cloth flour sack, if possible, and store it under our bed until the time of the big event.

On Halloween night, or maybe a few nights before – we usually fudged a couple of days – we would make our rounds. Although we did our Halloween pranks with other boys of the neighborhood, most of the time Monty and I found ourselves paired up together.

I don't know where the custom of throwing shelled corn at houses on Halloween night originated, but I do know that it sure provided us with a lot of fun.

For the uninitiated, the sudden raining chatter of shelled corn peppering the front porch and window panes, could be an unnerving experience, as was the case with one couple that lived in our neighborhood.

A day or so before Halloween and just after dark, Monty and I started our "Corning," as we called it. We started over on Acton Avenue, then worked our way back along Penning and eventually to Halloran. It was immediately after we had thrown a hefty handful of corn at a house on Halloran, that all hell broke loose.

Usually the biggest reaction to this kind of stunt was the man or woman of the house running out onto the porch and yelling into the darkness, "Alright, you kids! Stop that!" of course they couldn't see us, because by the time the corn hit the house, we were already high-tailing it for cover, or half way down the block.

The couple that resided in this particular house were immigrants who had only recently moved to this country – a consideration that never crossed our minds when we threw the corn at the front of their house.

After throwing the corn, we ran to the vacant lot across the street and jumped in an open pit, which had once been one of our many forts.

The couple came running out of the house yelling and carrying on as if we had thrown a live hand grenade into their living room. They were running around up and down the sidewalk, loudly yelling, "What's this!" "What's all this little golden stuff?" In their excitement, plus a very heavy Hungarian accent, it was almost impossible to understand what they were saying.

It was so dark in the field where we were hiding that we could probably have stood up and no one would have seen us, but we didn't. In fact, their reaction was so violent that we were not about to even peek over the edge of the pit.

Their loud outburst caused such alarm that shortly their neighbors were coming outside to see what was going on. Finally as their voices became calmer Monty and I finally built up enough nerve to stick our heads up and take a peak. We watched as neighbors were obviously explaining what, I'm sure, they thought was a very weird Halloween custom.

With much arm swinging and head shaking, they finally went inside and

Monty and I started breathing a little easier.

Many years later I gave this incident much thought and came to the conclusion that they took our little Halloween prank personally. Being immigrants and probably having known some personal persecution in their lives, they must have thought they were being singled out. Heck, what they didn't know was that Monty and I were non-discriminating pranksters, why, we even corned our own houses.

There were two other Halloween pranks that were very popular with our group during that period. One was sticking a car horn and the other was sticking a potato on the car exhaust pipe, both of which took a certain amount of courage.

To put a potato on the end of a car's exhaust pipe was not too difficult, but we had to be extremely careful to make sure no one was watching out the window.

We would case the target carefully, so to speak, by walking past nonchalantly, pockets bulging with potatoes. While one of us checked out the car, the other was watching the house. After we were satisfied that the coast was clear, the boy whose turn it was would slip up to the rear of the car and jam the potato over the end of the exhaust pipe, then slip away as fast and as quietly as possible.

The only problem with this stunt was that we were rarely around when the car was started and were unable to enjoy the results of our effort and never did know what the results were.

Now sticking horns was another matter entirely. On a still Halloween night, the sudden and constant blaring of a car horn, was a very unnerving experience to say the least, especially if you were the one sticking the horn. I only did this one time.

Monty and I had been corning on Penning, when we just happened to walk by a car that was parked with its windows open. We had not planned on sticking a horn that night, but this was such a perfect target, that we just couldn't let this opportunity pass.

The fact that we would find a car parked with its windows open was not unusual and perfectly illustrates the deterioration of the moral standards and social expectations since that period in our history.

Although automobile theft did occur in the 1930s, it was more rare than today and definitely unexpected. When it did occur, however, it was never the fault of the owner.

Today we are told to expect to have your automobile stolen and are judged culpable if we carelessly fail to abide by the rules established by our social progressives. These rules actually bestow a degree of moral right on the thief and a certain amount of legitimacy to the theft.

Another reason that cars were left with windows open was because of the lack of air conditioning. Drivers would usually leave their cars in that condition when they were parked except in inclement weather.

On this occasion we decided to try our hand at sticking the horn of this particular car. We had been with other boys when this was done, but neither Monty nor I had actually done it and always made sure we were a safe distance when the horn started blaring.

I don't know how the decision was made, but I was selected to do it. I know I wouldn't have unless the method of selection was fair and I could have saved face by refusing. Besides, Monty probably double, or triple-dared me.

The method of sticking horns is relatively simple. The main object is a nice springy stick, which would normally be prepared beforehand, about fifteen inches long and about one half inch in diameter. One end is positioned under the outer ring of the steering wheel, while holding the stick in the middle over the horn button. The stick would then be bowed upward in order to slip the other end under the opposite side of the steering wheel, then...when you have enough guts, let go and run lickety-split.

As I slipped up on the car, I was more nervous and scared than I'd ever been in my life (There would be other moments of fear later in my life, some maybe during the Korean War that may have equaled this, but I doubt it.) When I got to the side of the car, next to the driver's door, I just hunkered down and froze. I was sure I was not going to be able to pull it off. I was trying to think of any excuse I could that Monty would believe, but, there was none.

I finally built up enough courage to rise up and look through the open window toward the house to make sure no one was looking. I'd often heard Mom say, "Haste makes waste," so I knew I had to take my time if I was to do it right.

When I actually stood up and stuck my arms through the window, I was shaking like a leaf. I hurriedly stuck the stick under the steering wheel and then momentarily froze before I could release it.

Even though I knew what to expect, when I did finally let go, the sudden deafening blast from the horn almost sent me into shock. I know I must have stood there jumping up and down a few times before I could get my legs to propel me forward.

I took off down Penning and while I was still a half block away I could see

Monty going around the corner at Ninth Street, heading for Halloran. As I ran, that horn from hell seemed to follow me. I was giving it everything I had, but it felt like I was in one of my slow-motion dreams.

When I arrived at the corner of Penning and Ninth Streets, Monty was going around the corner at Halloran, heading for home. I ran diagonally across Halloran and followed him to his back porch where he was waiting. While sitting there panting and puffing, the sound of the horn, muffled by distance, abruptly stopped.

We continued to sit on his back porch steps in the dark for a while, excitedly talking while we caught our breath. It wasn't the run that had caused us to be so out of breath, it was the nervous excitement and fear. Sticking that horn was the big event of the night and I'm sure we both knew that throwing corn for the remainder of the evening would be anticlimactic. We called it a night and Monty went inside and I started walking home.

During the one short block to my house, I really felt good about myself, knowing I had overcome my fear and pulled it off, as punkish as it may have been. I also knew that I would never attempt it again.

Chapter XVII

Baked Chicken, à la Indian Style

The remainder of 1939 slipped by uneventfully. We still made our weekend excursions to Berry's or Reilley's Woods, or to one of the many other of our favorite haunts. On any given weekend, you could see anywhere from two to six boys of the Halloran group, trudging the many routes leading in and out of the Wood River area.

Our uniform of the day had now changed considerably. A few months earlier we would start out in the morning with only overall pants and sometimes shoes. Now we started out burdened down with jackets, caps, gloves, and of course shoes. Starting out on an early frosty morning, this extra apparel felt very comfortable and was worn very neatly. On the return, after a long hard day of play and the temperature had warmed considerably, we were hardly recognizable as the same tidy group, clipping along at a very crisp pace.

Returning, we would be staggering along at various speeds and intervals. Our stocking caps would be rolled high on our heads, or if we were wearing an aviator's cap, the ear and chin flaps would be snapped together on top, and the cap riding as high as possible. We would either have our jackets tied around our waist by the arms, or they would be dragging behind with the gloves stuffed in the pockets.

It was such a crew as this, while playing in the woods behind Reilly's farm one autumn day that acquired a sudden hunger for chicken, roasted on an open fire.

Farmer Reilly always had a large flock of chickens running loose all over the hillsides and woods behind his house. I personally know of a couple he lost but, other than those, I've often wondered how many he lost to hawks and foxes.

On this particular outing, we decided it would be fairly easy to catch one of the chickens in a flock that had wandered rather far from the house, back in the woods.

There were about six kids in our group from Halloran Avenue that day. Our strategy was hurriedly thrown together with each kid deciding how best we should go about it. We ended up with a consensus, more or less, to form a line and run through the flock to separate a few from the rest. We then would drive those few farther down into the woods where there was less chance for their cackling to be heard by people at the farmhouse.

Our strategy was simple enough, but catching one of those chickens was not. For the next thirty minutes I believe we covered all the woods behind Reilley, Berry and Vaughn's farms. We finally realized that one of the chickens was not quite as fast as the rest, so we concentrated all our efforts on that one chicken.

By the time we had cornered and captured that chicken, I don't know who was the worse for wear; us or the chicken. I do know we were scratched, skinned and a ragged looking lot.

For the life of me, I can't remember who was assigned the task of coup de grace, or how it was carried out. I only know that we now had one dead chicken on our hands and not the slightest idea of what to do with it.

We moved on down in the ravine farther away from the farm and started our fire. While the fire was building, we began debating on how best to prepare the chicken for roasting. Not yet boy scouts, none of us had the slightest idea of what to do.

The suggestion of cleaning it, which meant picking the feathers and gutting it – ugh, didn't set too well. It was when one of the boys spoke up and said "Let's cook it Indian style, whole with the feathers on and packed in mud," that we instantly and unanimously agreed.

Where the boy got the idea, or heard that Indians prepared their game in that fashion, I'll never know, but I soon began to doubt that Indians would be that dumb. Regardless, we were glad at the time that the decision had been made, because none of us wanted the icky job of gutting the chicken.

Several of us took the chicken to the creek and started packing blue mud around it. When we thought we had it sufficiently caked, it looked like a basketball.

We carried it back to the fire and placed it in the middle, then covered it over with more firewood. Ah yes, soon we would be dining on baked chicken, a la Indian style.

We continually fed the fire with more dry wood to make sure it stayed hot enough to do the job, occasionally poking the mass, or perhaps I should say mess, to see if the clay was hardening sufficiently.

Now each boy was voicing his personal opinion as to how long the chicken should remain in the fire. It appeared that we all had suddenly become experts at baking mud caked chicken on an open fire.

The caked mud had cracked in places and steam had been slowly spewing out for some time. We didn't let the smell of burnt feathers dampen our enthusiasm.

I don't know how long we let the chicken remain on the fire, but it really didn't matter. As it turned out, we could have timed it with the precision of a master chef, and the results would have been the same.

Finally, it was determined that it had cooked long enough. We were hungry and impatient to start feasting upon what we thought was going to be a treat. In our minds we visualized breaking the chicken open, pulling off tender drum sticks and cutting out large delicious hunks of breast, and eating it from bark plates that we had prepared.

As we rolled the ball from the fire with sticks, the hard baked clay started breaking apart. By the time we had rolled it about ten feet from the fire, all the clay had come loose. We all gathered around and silently stared down at the sodden mass of feathers, burnt in places, and with other substances oozing out here and there.

It immediately became clear after breaking the chicken open with sticks, why it was running a little slower than the other chickens; it was full of maggots.

We quickly turned away from the ugly glob and quietly went about the task of extinguishing our fire and then quickly left the area.

On the way home we slowly walked single file along the creek bed, trying to stay out of sight as long as possible. Although we played in those woods constantly without being run out or bothered, we still tried to avoid being seen by the landowners whenever possible.

It was in this very creek bed sometime later, that an incident occurred that Marvin and I still talk about. The creek bed was cut deep in places by the millions of gully washes that had passed along it. It was the funnel, the water shed, for this area on the north side of Vaughn's hill.

During dry spells with very little water, except in small pools, the graveled bottom served as our path in and out of the area.

The walls had deep undercuts in places with thick hairy tree roots hanging down, giving a dark, sinister, and spooky appearance. There was no telling what kind of monster was hiding up under those overhangs. We gave these areas a wide berth while passing.

On that particular day there were five or six boys in our group: Marvin and me, the three Stahlheber boys; Jack, Benny, Don, and possibly Monty. We were slowly and silently walking down the creek bed spread out in single file, heading back home after a hard day of exploring, as we called it, each deep in his own personal thoughts.

We had just cleared such an undercut in the bend of the creek when the silence was suddenly shattered by a high-pitched scream. Instinctively, we all spun around and momentarily froze in fright. Don came flying past us flailing his arms and wailing like a banshee. In unison, we took off, not knowing why and not about to stick around long enough to find out, but almost instantly knew the problem and scattered up the walls of the creek bed and took off in all directions. Don disappeared down the creek still yelling and slapping at a swarm of yellow jackets in hot pursuit. It was about ten or fifteen minutes and one-half mile later that we grouped up again. We came down off the hill and found Don waiting at the edge of the woods. He was whimpering and still rubbing at about a half-dozen stings. Marvin also had been hit a couple of times. The rest of us made it out clean.

Chapter XVIII

Hepcats and Jive-Talk

1939 came to a close and 1940 came in with a bang. World War II was raging in Europe. Germany invades Holland, Belgium, and Luxemburg. Italy declares war on England and France after Benito Mussolini joins forces with Adolph Hitler.

The battle of Britain began with a massive German air raid on South Wales. Less than a month later, Germany lost seventy-five aircraft in their largest air raid on England, and lost forty-five more over the English Channel a few days later.

On May 10, Chamberlain resigns and Churchill becomes Prime Minister of England. He makes his famous "Blood and Toil" speech a few days later.

German Panzers (armored divisions) encircle the British forces and were eventually cornered against the sea at the coastal village of Dunkirk. On June 4, 224,500 British and 113,000 French and Belgium forces were finally evacuated.

At home, President Roosevelt had closed all German Consulates and all aliens were required to register. The Fair Labor Standards Act went into effect, establishing the forty-hour work week.

The top songs of 1940 were: Blueberry Hill, Careless, God Bless America, I'll Never Smile Again, Indian Summer, Oh! Johnny, Playmates, Scatterbrain, South of The Border, When You Wish Upon a Star, and the Woodpecker Song.

The number one dance band in the country was Glenn Miller's. The top screen stars that year were: Mickey Rooney, Spencer Tracy, Clark Gable, Gene Autry, Tyrone Power, James Cagney, Bing Crosby, Wallace Berry, Betty Davis, and Judy Garland.

The Grapes of Wrath won the Academy Award for the best fiction, although it factually portrayed the misery during the dust bowl era in Oklahoma, Nebraska, and Kansas.

The best actor of 1940 was Jimmy Stewart in the Philadelphia Story. Best actress was Ginger Rogers as Kitty Foyle, and the best picture was "Rebecca."

There would be no Nobel Prizes awarded this year, nor would there be for the next three. The Pulitzer Prize in letters went to John Steinbeck for his novel, "The Grapes of Wrath."

From generation to generation, certain groups of people are identified either by the characteristics of their style of dress, behavior, or speech. Today we have the yuppies. In the sixties we had the hippies, and in 1940 we had the Hepcats.

Hepcats were a jivey bunch. They were in the groove; they were hep; they were cats; they were real alligators, and they couldn't tolerate an Ickie.

This was referred to as Jive-talk. Other words and terms used were: Canary – a female vocalist; the Eighty-Eights – a piano; licorice stick – a clarinet. To be in the groove meant to be carried away by the music. If you were Hep, you were on top of the latest swing music. Cats and alligators were words to describe themselves, and an Ickie was then what a Nerd is today.

To attain high fashion, the teenage girl bobbysoxers would mismatch their shoes and socks.

Of course, neither I, nor any of the boys in our group were old enough to get caught up in the latest fads. We had just arrived at the age when we started realizing that there were a few good qualities in girls. We had yet to hold a girl's hand, let alone dance with one.

* * *

During the bleak days of winter, especially on weekdays, we couldn't wait to get home to our favorite radio serials. There were several that we just couldn't miss, and they started about three thirty in the afternoon. This meant that we couldn't stop to play on the way home from school, or we would miss that baritone voice announcing, "It's Jack Armstrong!, the all American boy!"

As the radio announcer shouted those magic words and a male chorus would sing the "Hudson High Fight Song," we all began to live through another adventure of the bright, brawny, and reportedly pure-of-heart Jack Armstrong. He always led Hudson High to victory and of course asks all the little listeners to eat Wheaties.

Immediately after Jack Armstrong came Tom Mix. His cry was, "Reach for the sky! Straight shooters always win!! It pays to shoot straight!!!" And of course, he always encouraged us to eat lots of Ralston Wheat Cereal.

Among the many other radio serials we listened to were: The Lone Ranger, with a hardy, "Hi Oh Silver! Away!" The Green Hornet, Dick Tracy, and Buck Rogers.

Buck Rogers was a futuristic program, taking place in the year 2430 A.D. The writers and producers of that program never knew how fast their fictitious future would arrive. They missed their predictions of space travel by several hundred years.

Supposedly, when Macy's Department Store in New York City advertised that it had the Buck Rogers toy disintegrating guns, the next morning twenty thousand people were lined up for one-third mile, awaiting the store opening.

Later in the evening we would listen to a very spooky program called "Inner Sanctum Mystery." It would come on the air with a squeaky door opening very slowly. We would sit huddled together, not daring to make a sound. Then as the plot became more sinister, the voices would become lower and lower until they were but a whisper. Suddenly, the silence would be shattered by a terrifying scream, although expected, it would bring us up out of our chairs.

Except for the excitement of our after school serials, we were suffering from what is referred to as winter's doldrums. The days varied from bitter cold to chilly, damp, dreary, or windy. Temperatures ranged from a sunny fifty degrees one day to around zero the next.

Winters in the Midwest can best be described in one word – BLAH! There would be, however, several short periods when the snow would be deep enough and last long enough to provide us with joyous entertainment, especially on the weekends. We would stay out in it for hours and only go inside when we either became too wet, or our pants legs would be frozen stiffer than a board.

Our favorite spot to sled was on Dulaney Avenue, between Penning and Halloran. This stretch of road is almost flat now, but in the 1930's and 40's, there was an elevation change of four or five feet, starting at where the alley crosses Dulaney and sloping down to Halloran.

I realize that perspectives change as we grow older and become taller. Things that appear so large as children shrink in direct proportion to our increase in size; however, the law of gravity does not. We would never have congregated there on Dulaney and spent so many happy hours sledding if the slope had never existed.

Holding our sleds across our chests, we would run a few feet, then belly flop on them, then coast on across Halloran, or as far as conditions of ice and snow would allow.

Another proof that this rather abrupt slope did exist was an accident I had while coasting down it on a bicycle. I had only recently learned to ride and was still rather shaky and unsure of myself. The bicycle was old and in poor condition and I was unaware that the gooseneck of the handlebars was broken and would not stay in place.

As I coasted down Dulaney hill, I leaned back and as I did the handlebars pulled loose in my hands. I panicked and just sat there holding the handlebars straight out in front of me. I was picking up speed and heading toward Halloran, and I couldn't do a thing to stop it. I had enough presence of mind not to put on the brakes, knowing if I did I would go head first over the bicycle and land on the blacktop road surface.

I didn't have to think about it very long because the bicycle suddenly veered to the right and as it hit the sidewalk, the front wheel turned sideways and the bike flipped and sent me head over heels into a sandbur patch. I was not seriously hurt, however I had my t-shirt tacked to my back with about a dozen sandburs.

I don't know if the street department leveled that grade on Dulaney, or if a natural geographic change has taken place.

Chapter XIX

The Great Story Teller

After Christmas, winters seemed to last forever. January and February were always the longest months of the year. Each day passed grudgingly slow. Marvin helped considerably by keeping us entertained with his many fictitious stories of adventure.

Marvin found an old automobile steering wheel in a trash pile behind an automobile dealership. This steering wheel became the only prop he needed, around which to build many wild and wondrous tales.

Marvin became well known for his ability to spin a yarn. Most of the kids in the neighborhood had sat in on at least one of his performances.

On winter evenings or during the weekends, one or all of our cousins, Tommy, Bobby, or Veeda, would come over and we would gather in our bedroom for the big play.

There were times, of course when Marvin would exercise his total authority over the admittance and keep all girls out. This was never because of subject matter as much as it was just a – boy thing.

Marvin would sit on the bed with the steering wheel in his lap. He would hook one finger against a spoke and spin the wheel fast in either direction without using the other hand.

That steering wheel would become the control column of a bomber, taking us on an exciting raid over Germany. It might become the steering wheel of a powerful speedboat in pursuit of gangsters, or a racecar speeding around the track at the Indianapolis Five Hundred.

The stories that Marvin could build around that steering wheel were unlimited. He would include all the sound effects as well as the action as the story developed. If we were taking flack over Germany, he would include the "boom" and then bounce on the bed to simulate the concussion of a nearby

Ack-Ack burst. He would make all the sounds and motions necessary to give realism to his tale.

Anywhere from two to eight kids would sit staring wide-eyed and mouth open, totally enthralled while he extemporaneously and without hesitation weave an exciting tale of mystery and intrigue.

Marvin continued to entertain us with these exciting stories for the next several years. They seemed to stop about the time he reached his teens. I've always suspected that puberty is accompanied by more than just pimples; we seem to develop a severe case of self-consciousness as well – especially boys.

That steering wheel that received so much attention and gave so many hours of enjoyment, became just another item stashed under a bed and forgotten, though never discarded. Fifty-five years later, that steering wheel was found in Marvin's basement. The bakelite has cracked in places and the heavy wire skeleton is slightly exposed, but each time I would see it hanging there, I'd have flashbacks to the time on Halloran Avenue when it and Marvin provided those wondrous hours of entertainment so many years ago.

In 1995, I ask Marvin if he would loan me the steering wheel for a while, without telling him why. I took it and had it mounted in a shadow box on red velvet with a brass nameplate at the bottom with the inscription: "Marvin's Steering Wheel, Found in Wood River, Illinois -1940." I then surprised him with it on his 68th Birthday. It hung over his fireplace until his death.

I now have that steering wheel hanging on the wall in my office/library area where I look at it daily.

* * *

January and February finally passed and March came in like a lamb, which meant, according to saying, that it will go out like a lion – and it did.

Monty and I didn't much care how February came in, but did care how April came in, because for some weird reason that I've forgotten, it had become our tradition to go swimming on the first day of April. I'm not sure how long the tradition lasted, probably not more than a couple of years, but for those few years it was very important.

The first of April 1940 fell on a Monday which was a school day and meant that we would have to wait until the following Saturday to make our first plunge of the year.

The days were starting to warm up into the high fifties and sixties, which seemed like summer to us after the long, cold and wet winter.

Saturday morning broke clear, cold and calm. By about eleven o'clock it had warmed into the forties, but a stiff breeze came up and made the air uncomfortably cool.

It was about noon when Monty and I headed for Sones' pond. We walked up Vaughn's Road, to where the culvert ran beneath it. Taking our normal route, we cut down the east side, through the hazelnut thicket and continued along the edge of the creek all the way to the pond.

As we approached the levee, the sun was now at its summit and beaming down through the trees into the gully, causing us to shed out jackets.

As we crested the levee, we were greeted by a blast of cool air that made us shiver in out sweat-dampened shirts, causing us to hastily put our jackets back on.

We walked around the north end of the levee to where a large tree grew about twenty feet from the water's edge. We sat down and leaned against the tree and just stared at the pond.

The water was rather muddy looking, but that really didn't matter, it was that thin sheet of ice that extended about fifteen feet from shore that was causing our hesitation.

After sitting there for a while we decided that we would have to take a quick dip. We just couldn't let the tradition die, even if it had started the year before. We found a couple of long sticks and cracked the ice near the edge where we intended to enter. We swept the ice aside of the area as best we could, then hurriedly shed out clothing.

After two or three false starts, we finally got in as deep as our ankles, but only for a second before jumping back out. By running in and back out a few times, each time a little deeper, we eventually got in as deep as the waist.

By this time we had churned the water into what looked like liquid chocolate, which at the time mattered little. With a final burst of courage we ran out into the water and squatted down to our necks, then jumped up and ran out into the cold April wind and scrambled into out tangled clothes.

With our clothes damp from our wet bodies and out hair matted from the splashing, we ran down into the gully and out of the wind.

We located a warm protected spot from the gusty breeze and sat down to warm up and dry off. After a few minutes, we felt revived enough to start home. As we walked back down the creek through Vaughn's woods, we noticed our hair was matted into a sold crust. In those days, before modesty require that we carry a comb, we tried our best to pick wads of hair apart and use our fingers to comb it down the best we could.

We walked along Vaughn's Road with mud caked hair and brown streaks down our faces, neck and ears. Our pant legs and shoes were plastered with mud. After walking as far as Brushy Grove School, our toes were hurting so bad that we had to sit and clean the dried crumbling mud out of our socks and shoes.

I'll never forget the look on Mom's face when I entered the kitchen door. Although I had left my muddy shoes on the back porch and carrying my socks, Mom yelled, "What happened to you!" all the time pushing me back out the back door.

Mom had me strip down to my shorts out on the back porch. She picked up my muddy clothes and sent me to the bathtub. After I had cleaned up, or thought I had, Mom had to take me back and finish washing my hair over the sink.

*   *   *

Winter finally turned to spring and spring into hot summer. All summers were hot when I was a young boy, especially the nights. Our days were too full of play and excitement to be worried about such things. If we became too hot while playing during the day, we would find a nice shady tree to sit under and cool off for a while, then back at it again.

During July and August, it was the nights that gave us so much misery. This was long before air conditioning. The only means of cooling off was by electric fan, and there was usually only one per household.

Because Dad worked the night shift at the refinery, he always had the fan when he was sleeping, day or night. Many nights it would be too hot to sleep in a bed. We always tried to find the coolest spot in the house we could, and it would usually be on the floor. The two most favored spots were at the front or back screened doors. The only time the doors or windows were closed during the summer was when it was storming and blowing rain.

My favorite spot was at the back kitchen because the linoleum flooring was always cool, at least for a few minutes, and then I would have to move over a few inches to another cool spot.

Quite often we would sleep out on the front porch if the mosquitoes were not too bad. It was the buzzing I hated worse than the bites. I'd get so frustrated that I didn't care if they bit me, if only they would stop buzzing.

It was not uncommon for families, with their bedding, to drive to the parks and sleep on the ground during extremely hot periods. This was especially true in the parks in Alton.

The heat of summer was taken in stride by the boys of Halloran. To us it was playtime, and the heat, day or night, interfered little with our games. If we weren't playing baseball in the field between our house and Dulany Avenue, we were playing cork-ball in Paton's driveway, or possibly playing shinny, or tin-can hockey on roller-skates in the middle of the street, or just roller-skating.

Another game we played frequently was "Tippy." I've never seen this game played anywhere except in Wood River. The rules of the game are no longer clear to me, I remember it being played with a one-inch square piece of wood about four inches long and tapered to a point on each ends.

At night, we would play "Capture The Flag," starting just after dark and continuing until one side won, which sometimes was well after midnight. The center of our night games was usually the street light at Halloran and McHugh. If we weren't playing at the corner, we were sitting under it telling stories or, as we would say, "Shooting the Bull."

Our summers went by so swiftly. Although I was in the swimming pool almost every day, I never tired of it, and always felt sad and lost when it closed for the season.

Back to school again and another birthday, and without major incident, passed the remaining days of 1940.

Chapter XX

Unknown American Hero

1941 started out much like the previous year. The war was continuing to expand in Europe and now had spread to North Africa. General Rommel and his armored divisions had landed at Tripoli. Before the year's end the German and Russian alliance would fall apart and Germany would invade Russia.

The German forces started out sweeping over Russia so fast that it was predicted that they would fall by year's end. This proved however to be a false prediction. In fact this Eastern Front, as it was referred to, did in fact become Hitler's Waterloo.

The pride of the German navy, the Battleship Bismarck, was sunk by the British. England began their night air raids on Germany and Rudolf Hess defected the high German Command and flew to Scotland on a mission that was never fully explained..

On the home front, President Roosevelt was inaugurated for an unprecedented third term. In a speech to Congress, President Roosevelt introduced the term "Four Freedoms." Freedom of speech and expression, freedom of worship, freedom from fear, and freedom from want.

It was my understanding that the first two had been granted by the first amendment of our constitution. The third, freedom from fear, would be rather hard to pull off, and the fourth, freedom from want, was the beginning of the welfare state, as we know it today. In fact, four trillion dollars and one half century later, we've only nudged this one. Actually, we've taught later generations how to want.

No longer were we Americans to debate the fact that we were a neutral power after President Roosevelt signed the thirteen billion dollar lend-lease appropriations – all of it for war materials marked for use against Germany and Italy.

President Roosevelt ordered an embargo on shipments of scrap iron and gasoline to Japan and froze all their assets in the United States.

The Selective Service Act Extension was signed by the President on August 18, extending the length of military service to not more than thirty months and removed the nine hundred thousand man limit.

Industrial output was increasing at an incredible rate. A shipbuilding program of two hundred merchant vessels was called for by the federal government. Automobile production for domestic use had been cut by twenty percent in order to produce war machinery. The Office of Price Administration and Civilian Supply (APO) was established with limited power to recommend price controls, and a steel price freeze went into effect.

We were looking more and more like a nation preparing for the inevitable – WAR. The nation mourned the death of Lou Gehrig that year and the New York Yankee outfielder, Joe Dimaggio's record fifty-six game hitting streak came to an end on July 16.

Ben Hogan was golf's top money winner, Joe Louis defended his heavy weight title for the fifth time, and Whirlaway won the Triple Crown in horse racing.

The books that were being read in 1941 were: "Berlin Diary," "Random Harvest," "The White Cliffs of Dover," and "My Friend Flicka."

There would be no Pulitzer Prize in letter that year. For drama, the award went to Robert Sherwood for "There Shall be no Tomorrow."

The first television programming took place in 1941 when station WCBS in New York broadcast its news program on July first but it would be eight or ten years before the television became a common household appliance.

As the rest of the world fought each other, Monty and I continued to fight the battle of the varmints on the home front. There was hardly a daylight hour went by without seeing the two of us tramping through some field or woods, regardless of the weather.

Fox Grove, which was located at the northwest corner of Sixth and Edwardsville Road, was one of our spots to check out occasionally. This was a wedge of land of five to ten acres, covered with large oak trees and at the time we were convinced that its name derived from the fact that it was inhabited by foxes.

It was some years later that I learned it was actually named after a family by that name that had settled earlier in the Wood River area. During all our sorties into the grove, we only spotted a fox one time. The grove could very well have been called the owl patch, because we had spotted owls there frequently.

Monty and I rarely passed the grove while on our way to the airport without taking a detour through it. We just couldn't pass up the possibility that we just might spot Ol' Reynard.

The airport was located where the Sixth Street Park and Emerick Sports Complex now stands. In 1941 this airport, which was operated by the Soper Brothers, was a big attraction for the boys in the area.

With war activity on the increase, we began to see more and more military aircraft flying over and occasionally one would land for emergency reasons. When this occurred, we would run to the airport to get a closer look. The airport was less than one-half mile from Halloran, so it only took us a few minutes to get there.

The types of aircraft that would usually land were trainers, most likely from Scott Air Corps Base, located near Belleville, Illinois. We would get up as close to those aircraft as we dared to see and hear all we could. To stand close and listen to these young military pilots was the most exciting thing I could imagine doing.

If someone had asked me at the time to describe one of those airplanes, my reply would probably have been, "They're pretty." They were bright yellow overall with dark lettering on the side of the fuselage that designated which branch of service they belonged to, i.e., NAVY, or U.S. ARMY, and a large white star on a blue and red banner.

The most exciting moment was when they departed. We would wait for hours to watch them take off. If they had to remain overnight, we were always disappointed, because we knew we would probably miss the next day take-off.

The plane I remember most vividly was a T6-Texan. Whatever problem caused it to land was either fixed or inspected and found not to be major.

I watched closely as the pilot climbed up over the back of the wing and stepped into the cockpit. The greenhouse canopy, as it is referred to, was pulled back into the open position.

After he had settled into the seat, he finished buckling on his parachute, and then pulled his goggled cap over his head. He appeared to look down into the cockpit for the longest time, fiddling around with things. A few years later, I realized that what he was actually doing was going through his preflight checklist.

After what seemed like an eternity, but in reality was no more than five minutes or so, he was ready. He looked out the side of the cockpit to make sure he was clear, and then with his hand in the air, he gave a circling motion to indicate he was going to start the engine.

The propeller started moving as the engine gave a loud whine. It whirled a time or two, then slowed, then started with a big cough as the smoked bellowed out the exhausts. Within a couple of seconds, it was idling smoothly and had stopped smoking.

After one more look around the cockpit, he snapped his chinstrap. Looked up and out at us and with a salute started taxiing off toward the northwest corner of the field.

The field being all grass and uneven in places, he bounced a little, the wings shaking as he appeared to creep along to the end of the runway.

Once there, he turned into position and revved up his engine a couple of times then idled back and just sat there for at least a full minute. We were beginning to think he had another problem and was not going to go.

When we saw his canopy slide closed, we knew he was finally ready. The engine came up to full power and the plane started down the grassy runway. At first it appeared to bounce, but as the tail wheel came off the ground, it smoothed out and, within a few seconds, he lifted into the air. He had hardly cleared the ground by twenty feet when the landing gear started retracting.

As he climbed out to the southeast, crossing Ninth Street, he gave us a wing-wag – telling us goodbye. How little he knew at the time how much admiration he had created in a few young impressionable boys. He also could not have known that within less than a year he would be in the middle of a deadly war.

I often though about that young pilot during the war years and wondered how he fared. Did he go to the Pacific or European theater? Did he shoot down any Jap Zeros or German Messerschmitts and become a hero? Did he survive the war, or crash and die off some obscure Pacific Island.

Of course I would never know the answer to these questions, but as far as I was concerned, he would always be a hero to me.

After his departure, when the sound of the engine had faded in the distance, the airport seemed unnaturally quiet. There was an anticlimactic atmosphere as the few people working there silently resumed their normal daily routine.

As we walked back home, we walked through the watermelon patch that was growing adjacent to the south side of the airport, absentmindedly checking out the crop. We were known to come back at night and sample a melon now and then.

However, my mind was not on watermelons as we walked, I was still dreaming about flying and was determined that someday I would do it.

That dream came true some years later as I made my first solo while flying out of the Metropolitan Airport in East St. Louis, Illinois. The feeling of exhilaration and accomplishment was more than I ever thought it would be.

It would be impossible to describe the feelings and emotions I was experiencing as I drove home that afternoon with an entry in my flight log book that stated, "First solo this day, 21, Aug. 1956, by CFI A. E. Jones, 722280."

Chapter XXI

Resorting to Fisticuffs

It was during the summer of 1941 that Marvin and I had our biggest fight. Although we had had disagreements from time to time, they rarely developed into anything more serious than yelling, pushing and shoving.

Later, over the years whenever I'd recall that fight, I'd never been able to remember what Marvin did that made me angry enough to really take him on.

The incident occurred in the field directly behind Stahlheber's house. The usual group of boys had congregated just across the alley to pole vault at a stand we had built the previous year. It was made of a couple of rickety two-by-fours with nails spaced unevenly along the backside to hold the crossbar that was usually comprised of a limber fishing pole that sagged in the middle. Our vaulting pole was of heavy bamboo, about one and one-half inches thick with gobs of friction tape (the only kind available) to mend the many splits from heavy use.

Marvin and I may have started arguing over something as simple as whose turn it was – or maybe over something totally unrelated to pole vaulting. I do know I delivered the first punch, probably the only one I landed.

Marvin had me on the ground and was on top of me before I realized what had happened. He had me pinned to the ground and all my yelling, cussing, and kicking was of no avail. Marvin kept asking me to submit, which was pronounced "S'mit." With disgust and in humiliation I was forced to yell, "I s'mit" three times before he would let me up.

Marvin jumped off me, standing with his fist at the ready just in case I decided to take another poke at him. Hurriedly I jumped to my feet and started running toward home, crying and cussing to myself. About halfway down Stahlheber's driveway, out of site of the other kids, I stopped long enough to wipe my snotty nose and tear-stained face on my shirtsleeve.

While continuing toward home my anger and humiliation started resurfacing to the point that it was overcoming my good judgment. By the time I had reached the center of the street I could no longer restrain myself. I suddenly spun around, and with my head down like a charging bull, started running back as fast as I could go. As I came around the corner of Stahlheber's house, all the kids turned and looked in my direction and froze.

Although the distance I had to cover gave Marvin enough time to get ready, my speed and the fact that I would dare return caused enough surprise and shock that I was upon him before he had a chance to react.

I caught him full force with a body tackle and down we went with me on top, swinging my fists with everything I had. Marvin, while artfully dodging most of my blows, squirmed out from under me and immediately had me pinned once more. I must have gotten one or two good punches in because he was really mad now. He once again forced me to s'mit, but not before he bloodied my nose. This time he kept me on the ground until he was sure I'd had enough. For the second time I headed home crying and humiliated, but this time, with the addition of a bloody nose.

Out of sight around the corner of the house, I stopped again to wipe my face and daub my nose in the customary fashion – on my sleeve. By this time I was really beginning to look the worse for wear – clothes were disheveled and covered with dirt, shirt with blood streaks down the front, and face mud-smeared.

By the middle of the street I had almost made up my mind to try him one more time. Realizing I'd better leave well enough alone, I continued to our back yard and crawled under the grape arbor to sit awhile to soothe my wounded pride.

By the next day everything was back to normal except for my sore and scabby nose. Marvin, as it turned out, had a few scrapes and scratches as well.

*   *   *

The joyous days of that summer moved along much too fast. Each day was filled with ball games, hiking, swimming, or whatever other activity caught our fancy. The hot summer evenings, well into dark, were spent catching fireflies, playing capture the flag, or just sitting under the street light on the corner, shooting the bull.

Herb Paton, who lived across the street from us at 811 Halloran, had just become an Eagle Scout and was instrumental in getting me to join the Boy

Scouts. I joined just in time as our troop was attending a jamboree at the University of Illinois campus in Champaign the following week.

Mom was supportive of my involvement in Scouting and somehow came up with the five-dollar assessment for the trip. I never really thought I'd be able to attend because of the scarcity of money at home and was surprise when she gave it to me.

It was an exciting adventure, seeing troops from all over the state with their hundreds of pup tents pitched in every open space available on campus. Our troop was assigned a space out in the middle of the football field. I can't remember having any specific tasks or duties to perform while we were there. Most of the time was spent wandering around campus. I remember going into the gymnasium and sitting for a while watching the Illini basketball team practice, or at least that was who I assumed they were.

The most difficult experience I encountered during that trip was on the return when we stopped for lunch just outside of Effingham, Illinois. To this point in my young life, the only experiences I had at eating out were to sit at the counter of Reese's Drug Store, ordering a cherry coke, or at the Sunshine Café at the corner of Ferguson and Wood River Avenue, ordering a hamburger.

I had no experience whatsoever in ordering from a menu. The restaurant where we stopped was more than just a diner or greasy spoon. It was by far the fanciest eating establishment I had ever been in.

When we entered, we were led to a large round table accommodating about eight. Others in our group were seated at tables adjacent to ours. I was already starting to feel a little uncomfortable and out-of-place when the waiter came around with a water pitcher and menus.

I decided to follow the lead of the scoutmaster. Whatever he did, I would do. As he and the others picked up their menus and started to look at them, I did too.

As I began reading the menu, trying desperately to figure it out, I lost track of what was going on around me. I suddenly looked up and realized that the waiter and everyone else at the table were staring at me, waiting for me to order. Embarrassed, I quickly pointed at something and said, "I'll have that."

About twenty minutes later, after everyone at the table had their order of sandwiches almost eaten, my order of a one-half baked chicken with all the trimming was set down before me. Everyone stopped eating and stared at me as the waiter continued to set side dishes of vegetables around the plate of chicken. I could feel myself shrinking in my chair. If I could have slipped under the table and disappeared, I would have.

The first problem was trying hard to overcome my self-consciousness and embarrassment. The second was trying to figure out how to eat a one-half chicken. At home, Mom always cut it into pieces and fried it. It was a simple matter of picking up a drumstick and eating it.

I had hardly gotten started before all the other boys were done and either squirming in their seats or leaning back watching me eat. This, of course, only made it worse; I felt as if I was going to choke on every bite.

I may have forked the chicken a few times, but mostly I just wolfed down the vegetables as fast as I could. I finally decided to give it up and just sat there, waiting on someone to decide when to leave.

When I found out that the cost of my dinner came to almost a dollar-fifty, I was so thankful that I hadn't wasted all of the five dollars that Mom had given me on souvenirs while in Champaign. I did feel a little bad spending, or rather wasting, so much money, especially after I found out the other kids only owed about thirty or forty cents. I decided later that I wouldn't tell Mom about my dinning out experience.

During the summer of 1941, Mom and Dad decided to buy a house. Up to this time all the houses that we had lived in were rented. This news was accepted with about as much enthusiasm by us kids as it was when we first got the word that we were moving to Halloran from South Roxana. We had so woven our lives into the neighborhood on Halloran that the thought of leaving the area and our friends was unthinkable. It was only after we realized that it would only be eight blocks away and after we had looked over the house that the thought of moving became bearable.

*   *   *

As I sat in my car looking at the house at 834 Halloran, I struggled to force my thoughts back to the present, back from those warm childhood memories of nearly fifty years earlier.

It was with some sadness, not knowing if I'd ever return, that I started the car, eased around the corner and headed for Sixth Street. I took the opportunity for one quick glance at the homes of my childhood friends as I passed by.

I turned right at Sixth Street and then left on Beach and continued five blocks to the intersection of Beach and Leslie Avenues. I pulled around the corner to the right and stopped in front of the house at 501 Leslie.

HUCKLEBERRY HEART:
THE BOYS OF HALLORAN AVENUE

This was the first house that we had ever purchased. It was Spanish stucco, located on the corner of Beach and Leslie Avenues. It had a fireplace and a crystal chandelier hanging in the dining room. It undoubtedly was the nicest house that we had lived in, although it seemed out of place in a neighborhood with only wood-frame houses.

After the move we still carried on our daily activity with the gang on Halloran, as if we had never left. After all, what's eight blocks to kids who routinely hike miles? However, after a period of time, as a new circle of friends developed, those eight blocks slowly became a buffer and diminished the frequency of contact with the old gang. Although we continued to meet or run into each other around town, at school, or at the swimming pool, our planned hikes and outings became more rare. "The Boys of Halloran" slowly grew apart.

Monty Heffner and I were still very close, but that too was soon to change for a short period. Monty had moved east of Ninth Street, which meant that he would now have to attend the Roxana school district during the coming year.

When school started that fall it was not the same without Monty sitting somewhere behind me where we could whisper back and forth, plotting and scheming our next adventure.

It wasn't long though before another boy and I became close friends. Although Monty and I still buddied around together occasionally, it was Bucky Walters and I who were closest for the remainder of that school year.

I was still in the Boy Scouts working on my merit badges whenever the mood struck me. During a warm fall Saturday, Herb and I went up in the woods behind the cemetery to work on one of my badges. He was to verify that I could cook meat on an open campfire.

I was required to make fire and then build a holder for the meat out of green sticks. I had to find the right size forked sprout that when trimmed properly would allow the fork to be brought together at the top and tied. With this round loop now formed, I had laid a couple of small sticks on top upon which I laid the steak. Two other small sticks were woven across the top to hold the meat in place. When held up it looked like a small crude tennis racket with a steak in the middle. Needless to say, I won my merit badge that day.

December 6, 1941 was a big day for our Boy Scout troop. We headed to our winter Jamboree at Pere Marquette State Park just northeast of Grafton, Illinois. We were excited about getting to stay in small cabins that held about eight boys in double bunks. A small pot bellied stove was in the middle of the room to provide warmth and one naked light bulb hung from the ceiling.

When we arrived Saturday morning, the place was already alive with activity. Many of the troops had arrived the night before and were staying three nights. It's my recollection that we were planning on staying through Monday morning. I'm not sure how we worked that out, with Monday being a school day, but it sure was OK with me.

Our troop spent the rest of the day getting settled in and becoming acquainted with our surroundings. That night one of the assistant scout leaders came to our cabin, and as we boys lay around on top of our bunks, he told ghost stories.

It was a perfect setting for telling ghost stories, especially when someone was good at it. The room, even with a small fire in the stove, was chilly. The one very low wattage bulb hanging in the center of the room cast dark shadows in the corners and behind the bunks.

As the leader spun his long tale of three young men lost in a large haunted house, his voice started becoming quieter and quieter as he described how in later years each of the young men started going mad. After about fifteen minutes into the story, he had all of us hanging on to his every word in petrified suspense.

After telling slowly how the first two young men had gone crazy in an agonizing way, his voice had lowered to but a whisper. While all of us were straining to hear, he finished by whispering slowly, "And there is only one – man – left," then total silence for about ten seconds, as he stared wide-eyed into the face of every boy. He then jumped straight up out of his chair and screamed at the top of his lungs, "I'M NOT CRAZY AM I!!!!" Every boy in the hut jumped straight up in their bunks and screamed as loud as he did. It took us a good five minutes to come down off the ceiling. If we had had claws, Sylvester the Cat would have had nothing on us. There may have been a boy or two that needed to change their drawers.

Finally we settled down for the night and crawled under our blankets, but no one volunteered to get up and turn off the light, nor did anyone suggest it.

We awoke the next morning, December 7th, to a bright cold sunny day. The ground that had thawed and become muddy the day before was once again frozen with frost heaves.

It was about midmorning when our troop took off on a hike through the park. We hiked in a large circle through the woods and came back along side a stream. The sun had warmed the frozen path, making it very slippery, causing one boy to slip and slide into the water up to his knees. While trying to scramble up the muddy bank his feet came out from under him and he slid back in on his stomach. Now, not only was he soaked from above his knees, but the front of his jacket and pants were caked with a solid layer of mud. With the help of the troop leader and some of other boys he was finally pulled up the bank. He really looked pitiful, walking stiff legged back to camp. Some of the boys started calling him Frankenstein.

We had only been in camp a few moments before we heard the news. Someone shouted, "The Japs bombed Pearl Harbor!"

Dorothy (Irey) Isom - Author's mother circa-1923

John Nelson Isom - Author's father circa-1927

Gene Nelson Isom - Marvin James Isom - 1930

TOP: *Author and wife Doris, visits his old home*
834 Halloran Avenue - 2001
BOTTOM*: Fern Irey, Dorothy Irey Isom, Norma Irey, Wave Irey*
Circa 1914

Back row -Marvin Isom, Tommy Lawrence, Dorothy Worthington, The Author, Veeda Worthington

Front row - Norma Isom, Jack Isom, Rita Isom
Circa - 1939

Author - Gene Nelson Isom - Age 16

TOP: *Back row - Ralph Crawford, Jack Stahlheber, Ben Stahlheber, Bill Scoggins Front row - Don Stahlheber, Mariam Ritter, Bobby Ritter, Ralph Scoggins Dog - Trigger Paton circa -1938*

BOTTOM*: Marvin Isom, Herb Paton, Gene Isom - circa 1939*

TOP: *Towboat Vagabond, the boat the author left Wood River on in 1945*

BOTTOM: *Marvin Isom's steering wheel*

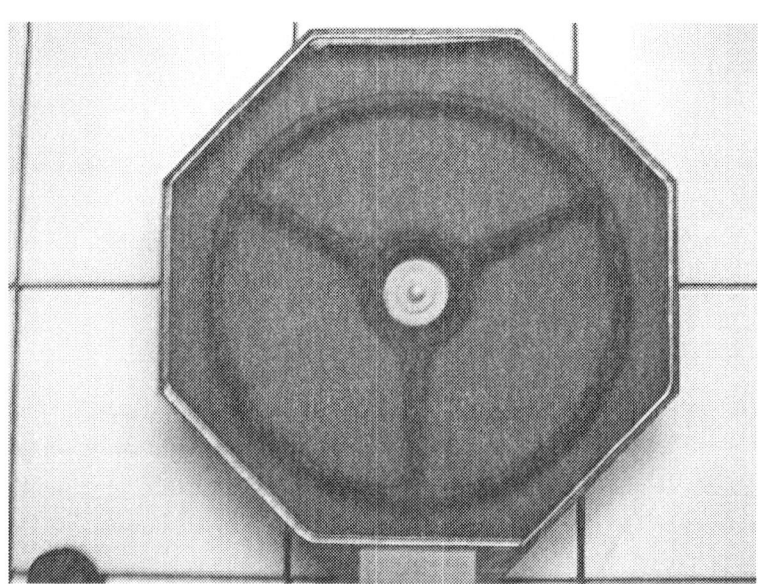

Chapter XXII

Pearl Harbor

Yes, the news was out. The word that the Japs had made a sneak attack on Pearl Harbor was all over the camp. Everyone was scampering around trying to listen to the few radios available. Most of the young scouts assembled had never heard of Pearl Harbor and hadn't the slightest of idea of what a Jap was, but in just a few short days they were about to become very informed.

Needless to say, our jamboree was about to come to a very abrupt end. Many of the scout leaders were members of the military reserves and needed to report to their various units as soon as possible.

We immediately started packing our things and within a very short time we were on our way home. Pere Marquette State Park was only about twenty-five miles from where our troop headquarters was located near the Colonial Dairy on Ferguson Avenue in Wood River.

From Ferguson Avenue to where we lived on Leslie was about ten blocks. Walking home with my bedroll and other gear, sometimes half dragging it, I knew Marvin would be listening to the radio and would bring me up to date as soon as I got home.

Sure enough, Marvin had been listening to the news constantly since he first heard the report earlier in the day. He was listening on a brand new radio that Dad had bought and put away as a Christmas present, but immediately took it out of the box as soon as they heard that the Japs had bombed Pearl Harbor.

I joined him and he brought me up to date on everything that he had heard so far. Although we were concerned, we really didn't understand the total consequences of this sneak attack on America. The excitement and invincibility of youth protected us from the fear that I'm sure most older people were experiencing as a result of this attack.

The three attacks on Pearl that morning was devastating. The Japanese sank the U.S. Battleships Arizona, California, Oklahoma, and the Utah, and would have gotten our aircraft carriers as well, had they been in port that morning. They destroyed most of the Army Air Corps while still on the ground at Hickam and Wheeler fields.

On board the U.S.S. New Orleans at Pearl during the attack, Chaplain Howell Forgy told the gun crews he was sorry that they didn't have church that morning but to "Praise the Lord and pass the ammunition."

When the news of the attack was received in Washington, Navy Secretary Knox, blurted: 'My God!, this can't be true, this must mean the Philippines."

"No Sir," said Admiral Stark, "This is Pearl."

Edward R. Murrow had been invited to dine with the President that evening. His wife called to ask if it was still on. Eleanor Roosevelt said, "We have to eat; come anyway." Later that night President Roosevelt pounded the table as he described how our planes were caught on the ground.

The Japanese not only attacked Pearl Harbor, but the next day, on December 8, they also made land and sea raids on Hong Kong, the Pacific Islands of Guam, Wake, and Midway, plus a large scale invasion of the Philippine Islands.

Although we had just become involved in what would be the biggest war the world had ever known, there were some who were more interested in trivial pursuits. Some people were calling newsrooms around the country trying to find what the score was between the two Chicago football teams, the Bears and the Cardinals. "Ain't you getting anything besides that war stuff," they'd ask.

On December 8, the United States declared war on Japan and President Roosevelt made his famous "Day of Infamy" speech to the nation, and on December 11th, we declared war on Germany and Italy.

On December 24th, Christmas Eve, a small but heroic garrison of Marines had to surrender the island of Wake, after holding out for days against a huge Japanese invasion force.

By early 1942, we were in one of the biggest military buildups in history. Immediately after Pearl Harbor, the military services started recruiting and drafting troops faster than they could process them. By the end of the war, there were sixteen million Americans in uniform.

War posters were popping up everywhere. There was not a post office or government building anywhere that did not have a poster out front depicting Uncle Sam staring at you sternly with his finger pointing and a caption that read, "Uncle Sam Wants You. Enlist Now."

Another poster seen everywhere was a gloved hand turning a nut with a wrench – caption, "America's Answer! Production!" Other posters frequently seen had a group of female factory workers standing in work coverall with a caption that read: "Soldiers Without Guns!" In addition, another depicted the arm and hand of an American worker grasping a serpent with oriental eyes.

It wasn't long after the war started that little banners with stars began to appear in windows of homes all across the nation. They showed one star for each member of that household serving his/her country in uniform. By the end of the war, hundreds of thousands of those little stars had turned GOLD, indicating that that member had been killed in the defense of our country.

Everyone was going into action. Cartoon characters were involved as well. Superman, although declared 4-F because of his x-ray vision, spent the war pushing the Red Cross and V-bonds, the V standing for Victory. Smilin' Jack joined the air force. Terry fought the Japs instead of the pirates. Daddy Warbucks served as a general, while his adopted waif, little Orphan Annie, exhorted real kids to collect scrap metal, and Joe Polooka became a private in the army.

Hollywood was doing its part as well. They started pitching in with many patriotic war movies, always depicting the villains as sadistic Germans, bumbling Italians always in retreat, or wily bucktoothed Japanese.

Some of the more famous movies were "Purple Heart," "Above Suspicion," "Keep Your Powder Dry," "Five Graves to Cairo," and ""Air Force."

If you were into music during 1942, you sure got an earful. Some of the novelty songs that year were: "Rosie The Riveter," "G. I. Jive," "This is The Army Mr. Jones," and "Der Fuehrer's Face."

Radio and juke boxes were playing ballads like: Lilli Marlene," still a favorite among soldiers of all nations since World War One; "White Cliffs of Dover," "When The Lights go on Again;" "I Left my Heart at The Stage Door Canteen;" and "Don't Sit Under The Apple Tree."

Four of the more inspirational songs during this period were: "He Wears a Pair of Golden Wings," "Johnny Got a Zero," "Roger Young," and probably the one heard most often, "Praise The Lord And Pass The Ammunition."

During January, 1943, the WPB (War Planning Board) issued Directive Number One. This directive instituted rationing. This came as a shock to a nation unused to any kind of rationing or controls. We were suddenly stuck with little books of stamps that determined the amount of food and gasoline could we buy.

Gasoline rationing was especially unpopular. The Average driver was issued an "A" Card, limiting it to three gallons of gasoline a week. At first, this created much cheating, but eventually most citizens made do with the "Patriotic" three gallons.

Almost everything we liked to eat became rationed – meat, coffee, sugar, butter, and cheese. The point system almost drove housewives, as well as the grocers, crazy.

Officials of APO had devised what they thought was a workable plan. The ration books contained stamps of different point value, according to color. All grocery items on the shelves were labeled with the number of points as well as the price per pound. Porterhouse steak, for example, cost sixty-one cents per pound and 12 ration points. This meant that you would have to forfeit two of the red or blue stamps with a value of ten points each, and receive in exchange eight red or blue tokens, which had a value of 1 point each.

In practice however, this system turned out to be a big chaotic snafu. (Snafu was an acronym used quite frequently during those war years, however, its meaning can not be explained here.) Yet during the war the citizens of the United States were fed better than ever before. By 1945, the last year of the war, the Department of Agriculture reported that Americans ate more food and spent more money on "Victuals" than at any other time in history.

To supplement the scarcity of raw materials needed for the war effort, the nation went on the biggest scavenger hunt in history. Everyone was going through their attics, basements, and trash piles, looking for old rubber overshoes, rusty baby carriages, old metal pots, pans, tin cans and anything else that could be turned into armaments or other needed war material.

So successful was this national scrap drive that, at first, the Government could not handle the load. The piles of debris sometimes accumulated for months before it could be moved and processed. By June of 1942, the Boy Scouts waste paper drives so glutted the paper mills that the drive had to be temporarily suspended.

Even though we were in the midst of a great war, politics went on as usual. The Democrats and Republicans still fought it out on Capital Hill over social issues. Of course, the President was a Democrat, as well as most of the country. Although each party used whatever political clout they had to try to gain control of the seat of power in Washington, they were totally united in defeating the Axis. Unlike today, we had only one Tokyo Rose in those days, and she lived in Tokyo. What dissension existed within the United States at that time, were so overwhelmed by unity, that their voices were heard by few.

An example of the strength of the entrenched Democrat Party can best be understood by a political cartoon of the day. The cartoon depicted high society matrons at a cocktail party. One is saying to the other, "Why don't you become a Democrat and start enjoying politics?"

The contrast between the 1940s and 1990s is striking. Today, Democrat politicians are switching to the Republican Party by the hundreds. Is this what is meant by an old saying that I've heard all my life – "What goes around, comes around?" It does prove one thing, nothing is static in politics.

Whether the news was about politics or about the war, Marvin and I listened intently. We couldn't wait to hear the broadcasts of Walter Winchell, Gabrael Heater, or Edward R. Murrow. Walter Winchell started his broadcasts with – "Hello Mr. and Mrs. America, and all ships at sea." Gabrael Heater always let us know immediately if there was "Good" or "Bad news" to report that night. At the beginning of the war almost every night he would start his broadcasts on a note of sadness – "Oh, there is bad news tonight." Later, after our forces were starting to make some advances – after Colonel Doolittle's raid on Tokyo, Japan, on April 18th – he started with, "Oh there is good news tonight." Those were the reports we were always looking forward to because they always lifted our spirits.

Edward R. Murrow, who made his headquarters in London, would come on the air with a deep resonant voice—"This is London calling," and give us all the up-to-the-minute war news.

If we were interested in gossip or what the movie stars were up to, we could always listen to Jimmy Fiddler, who started his program with "Flash," then gave us the latest scandal or other news concerning the Hollywood scene.

By the middle of 1942, the news was starting to become less depressing. We were starting to win a few very important battles, both on land and sea. These victories were received with much celebration, after two disasters: First, Bataan fell to the Japanese on April 9th and the subsequent Death March resulting in the deaths of 5200 American soldiers; and, Second, on May 8th the Japanese took Corregidor following the surrender of American forces commanded by General Wainwright.

On May 8th, the battle of the Coral Sea ended with seven Japanese warships sunk by United States carrier-based airplanes. Less than a month later, on June 6, the battle of Midway ended with the United States fleet sinking four Japanese carriers and thirteen other ships.

The United States Marines landed on Guadalcanal in the Solomon Islands on August 7, in the war's first American amphibious operation.

The war was having an effect upon the home front in many ways. One that affected us in a personal way, was the price of real estate. After having owned our house on Leslie Avenue for barely a year, its value had increased to a point that Dad (shortsightedly) decided that he would sell it for the profit. So once again, during the summer of 1942, we up and moved to a rented house, in Glendale Gardens.

*   *   *

As I drove away from the house at 501 Leslie, I continued north on Leslie and drove around the curve and turned right onto 2nd Avenue. When I came to Edwardsville Road, I turned right again and headed east.

Driving alone the road that we used to refer to as Vaughn's Road, I became disoriented and confused. This was not the road that had fronted our house when we lived here. It was only after I had pulled into the Wal-Mart parking lot, at the Wood River Center, that I was able to regain my bearings.

I had some trouble finding my way back into Glendale Gardens. I backtracked to 13th Street, and came into Glendale Gardens by way of Midway Street. As I drove slowly along I couldn't believe the changes that had taken place.

When we moved here, back in 1942, the area was sparsely settled. There were many lots and even whole blocks that were vacant. I should know – this is where I joined the steadily employed – delivering newspapers. Day after day for months I would walk these streets making my deliveries.

Today as I drove, I passed a house that I remembered well, because it was there that I always had trouble collecting. I could rarely catch the subscriber home and when I did, he always tried to short-change me.

Turning left on Greenview Street and then right at the corner, I stopped in front of the house at 437 Harrison Street. This was it, our old home, but oh how things had changed. Although the house looked much the same, everything surrounding it was different. When we moved here, the house was located on a five- acre lot.

New houses now stand near it in the pasture where cows once grazed. The landlord used to keep eight or ten head of cattle on the property. We made a pet out of one baby calf. We named her Cookie and let her run in the yard. She would run and play with us just as a dog would. I recall when she would lie in the sun on warm spring days and we would lie down beside her and use her as a pillow. I still remember the soft feel of her fur.

From the front yard, we could look across Vaughn's Road and see nothing but open fields all the way to Vaughn's Ridge. The only structures that could be seen from Vaughn's Road to Ninth Street were the three farms of Vaughn, Reilley, and Berry.

Because of the openness of Glendale Gardens, we used to feel like we were in the country. Vaughn's Creek ran just one block east and the woods were less than a quarter-mile away.

All the fields to the east and north of Glendale Gardens were planted in crops of wheat, corn, or soybeans. Where the firehouse now sits used to be an open field, bounded on the north and south by Midland Street and Vaughn's Road, usually planted in wheat.

Now that we were living in Glendale Gardens, we were back in the Roxana School District. This meant that Marvin and I had to walk a little more than a mile to the Roxana School. There were no school buses in 1942, which made it rough on days when the temperature was near zero and a strong wind blowing. I can remember days when Marvin and I would walk backwards or sideways almost all the way to school and back to keep our faces out of the sharp wind. Thank God for the energy of youth.

Rita, Norma and Jack were more fortunate. They attended Brushy Grove School, located only four or five blocks away.

Attending the Roxana School had at least one plus though, it meant that Monty and I were back together in the same classroom and I believe the same old seating arrangement.

The family quickly adjusted to living in Glendale Gardens, especially us kids. We were living in a completely different environment than any previously. It was like living on a farm in the country, but with all the convenience of urban living.

With cattle on the property and the chicken house and other outbuildings to play in, it was truly an exciting place to be. Many residents in the area raised chickens or other livestock. On the property just south of us, people raised milking goats.

Marvin and I spent a lot of time that first summer playing and exploring the area. Although we were very familiar with Vaughn's Creek and Woods, we could spend more time there now than before we moved because it was virtually in our back yard.

It was while we were fishing and playing at the creek that runs under Vaughn's Road, that Marvin broke his arm. The large concrete drainage viaduct that ran under the road was our thoroughfare for crossing from one side to the other. The only problem was a high retainer wall on the west side to prevent debris from clogging the viaduct. This wall held back enough water to form a small fishing hole.

I had just dropped down from the top of the wall and was going through the viaduct and Marvin began to follow. When I heard him yell I turned around to see what had happened. He was standing, holding his arm and groaning. Returning to him, I asked what happened, and he yelled, "I broke my arm!"

Of course I didn't really believe he had actually broken his arm. As kids, we usually exaggerated our hurts and pains and I was sure that was what Marvin was doing. When I reached him, however, I knew he wasn't kidding. He was cradling his right with his left. As I looked down at it, I couldn't believe what I saw. His arm from elbow to wrist was in a shallow vee. As we stood there his arm slowly straightened out as if it was made of hard rubber. He told me that when he first looked at it, it was real bad but immediately started straightening.

I scampered back up the wall and gathered our fishing gear while Marvin went on through the viaduct to come out on the other side of the road. In his condition, there was no way he could get back up the wall.

Marvin cradled his arm all the way home and made me swear not to tell Mom or Dad. He had broken his arm once before while living in South Roxana, and could remember too well how much it hurt when the doctor had to set it, and was not about to go through that again if he could help it.

Marvin suffered with that broken arm for weeks before he could use it comfortably. Luckily, he is left handed, or he would not have been able to make it, especially in school.

We kept his secret and he was able to hide it and bluff his way through. I believe it may have been many years later, after we were grown, before Mom learned of it.

Chapter XXIII

Mexican Stand Off

In the middle of the summer, Marvin, I and the Stahlheber boys got together and planned a big overnight hike to Indian Creek. Although we had spent many days hiking the Indian Creek area, this was the first time we had actually planned to spend the night.

After much planning and preparations, we started out early one morning, weighted down with all the supplies we thought we would need: bedrolls, tarps, pots, pans, food, canteens, and toilet paper. We actually had more than we could comfortably carry.

As we trudged up highway 143, the hard road as we called it, the morning sun was already starting to make itself felt. It was around eleven o'clock by the time we arrived at where the road crosses the creek.

We left the highway and walked up the creek for about one-half mile, to a spot where we had played and swam before. It was a spot with large shade trees and flat grassy ground ideal for camping. The area was pastureland and the cattle kept it well mown.

After a refreshing swim and long rest we prepared our camp and spent the remainder of the day hiking and running around the woods, playing Indians and having a great time.

At dusk, we built our fire and cooked hotdogs and roasted marshmallows. By the time it was completely dark, we quietly sat around our campfire, totally exhausted from the day of activity.

It was during this tranquil period that we were suddenly startled by a loud voice from out of the darkness that shouted, "Hey, you boys! Get the hell out of here!" Needless to say, his abrupt and harshly yelled words literally scared the hell out of us. He obviously had seen the light of our campfire and had come to investigate.

We probably mumbled some kind of apology and quickly started gathering our gear. After putting out the fire, we left the area, never having seen the man who had yelled at us, looking nothing like when we arrived. Our once neatly rolled bedding was now slung over our shoulders. The rest of our equipment was tucked under our arms as we struggled through the darkness to the highway.

After arriving back at the bridge on route 143, we huddled to decide what action to take and reorganize our gear. Thank goodness for what little moonlight there was; it helped considerably. If it had been the dark of the moon, we would have been in deep trouble.

Not having another campsite in mind close by, we finally decided to go all the way back home and sleep in the haystack across from our house, but instead of going back by the road, we decided to take a shortcut across country. Boy! Did this turn out to be a major blunder. Not only was it not a shortcut, but also turned out to be an incredible obstacle course, through fields, over fences, down through gullies and woods – all in the dark.

It was while going through a field of wheat stubble, that we flushed a covey of quail almost out from under our feet. Even though we knew instantly what they were, the suddenness of loud fluttering wings in the stillness of the night, was enough to put us all into momentary shock. We thought the haunts had us for sure.

Eventually we came onto Vaughn's Road at the viaduct and walked down to the wheat field, then cut across to the haystack. Once there, we threw our equipment down and just flopped, then crawled up on top and snuggled down in the hay, prepared for a good night's sleep, or at least what was left of it.

By the time we had reached the haystack, it was at least two or three in the morning. The day had truly been an exhausting test of our endurance. That alone should have been what made this experience unforgettable, but it wasn't. It was what happened while we lay there looking up into a brilliantly clear star-filled night that caused memories of that night to be permanently etched in our minds.

We had just settled down when someone shouted, "Hey, there goes a shooting star!" As we lay there looking up, we soon saw another, then another, and within a few moments, we were seeing two at once. During the next hour or so, we witnessed the most spectacular meteoroid display that we had ever seen, before or since.

We didn't know it at the time, but we were witnessing the Perscid meteor shower, which occurs between the first and second week of August each year.

It is believed to be the disintegrated remains of Tuttle's comet, first identified in 1862.

Marvin and I have watched for this shower of meteoroids many times since and have yet to see a show as spectacular as the one we experienced that August night in 1942.

Suddenly I awoke with a bright sun shining in my eyes. I didn't remember getting sleepy, but sometime during the meteor shower, I drifted off. As I collected my wits and looked around, boys were curled up in crevices and depressions all over the top of the haystack.

After everyone had been aroused, we slowly and quietly gathered up our belongings and after saying we'd see you later, headed for home. Little did we know as we walked home that morning, that fifty years later, the spot where we had spent the night would be in the middle of a Wal-Mart parking lot.

Haystacks were a part of the landscape in those days. The day of the combine was yet to come, or at least to be widely used. Most all wheat had to be cut, bundled and shocked (stacked) before it can be thrashed.

The huge steam driven thrashing machines were strategically placed near to, or, in the corner of the field to be thrashed, and wagons would haul the wheat to the machine. The huge piles of straw (haystack) were the result of the machine separating the grains of wheat from the chaff.

These haystacks would remain for days or weeks until they were disposed of. In some fields, haystacks remained for years, settling and becoming an ugly dark gray mound, but while they were fresh and clean, they made wonderful play areas for kids.

The location of the Glendale Gardens Fire Station is the area where they usually set up the thrashing machine for that wheat field. This meant of course that each year there would be a new haystack on that spot in which we kids could play.

The haystack at that location in 1942 had been standing only a couple of days before Rita, Norma, Jack and a couple of their friends started playing in it. The hay, because it was so slick, made it difficult to climb to the top of the stack. This is also why they made such wonderful slides. The haystacks after settling, would become like thatch, making it possible to build tunnels or caves in them.

It was while my sisters and brother, and their friends were playing in this fashion that the haystack caught fire.

Norma had removed her leg brace and laid it aside at the base of the stack.

Jack just happened to look over and see smoke arising next to Norma's leg brace. He ran over and pulled the brace away from the small fire that had started. The kids started yelling and running. Norma quickly scrambled to where Jack had laid her brace and hurriedly put it on while the kids kept yelling, "Hurry up, Norma, hurry up!"

As the haystack burned, the kids ran toward home, hesitating momentarily to urge Norma on, who by now had strapped on her brace and was running stiff legged after them.

By the time they had gotten a block or two away, the stack was a burning inferno, flames shooting a hundred feet in the air. After only a few minutes the only thing remaining was a heap of black smoldering ashes and a huge cloud of white smoke hanging over northeast Wood River.

Rita, Norma, Jack and their friends finally made it home. They scampered inside and hid, hoping no one would find out they did it.

However, they obviously had been seen. A few hours later, there was a knock on our door and there stood the landowner of the wheat field. He questioned whether the kids had been playing with matches and had mischievously burned down his haystack. They at first tried to deny they were there, then confessed, but swore they had not been playing with matches.

Nothing came of the incident. Mom and Dad were not made to pay damages and the incident eventually passed and was forgotten, except for the memories.

To this day, they still maintain their innocence. Of course, the cause is obvious to us now. Disaster was sure to happen with a hot August sun bearing down on a bright shiny stainless steel brace on very dry straw. The reflection of the sun off that shiny metal acted as a magnifying glass, causing the combustion.

*   *   *

Marvin and I still visited Tommy quite often because he still lived in South Roxana and we never tired of playing in and exploring the Grassy Lake area.

It was during one of these trips that we happened to discover young catfish hatches in a small pond toward the end of the marshes. We were very fascinated with the thick black schools that would boil to the surface then sink again out of sight, only to boil up again a short distance away. They had just hatched and were no longer than an inch in length.

Monty Heffner was with us on that occasion and came up with the idea of transplanting some of the catfish hatchlings into Sones' Pond. Now at first thought this seemed to be a great idea and we all agreed of course, giving little thought whatsoever as to what the owner of the pond may have thought about it.

We ran back to Tommy's house and hurriedly returned with a bucket and tub. Using the bucket, we took turns wading into the pond, no deeper than our waist, and slowly slipped upon the schools of baby catfish. It was a matter of timing and luck to be in the right position when the school surfaced. We were successful often enough to eventually scoop up hundreds of catfish.

With our tub half full of water and fish, we started out on what was to become one of the hardest tasks that we had ever undertaken. Had we had thought this project through thoroughly before we got underway, it would never have happened.

It was probably around one o'clock in the afternoon when we left Grassy Lake and headed for Sones' Pond. We started out with two of us carrying the tub, stopping to switch hands every hundred feet or so. With only three of us—Tommy was unable to go with us because of some other commitment—one boy rested while the other two carried, then we would rotate.

By the time we had come abreast of the Shell Oil Refinery main gate, we knew we were in trouble. Having gone just a little over a mile with about three to go, we were not at all convinced we could make it.

The tub gradually became lighter as we slouched our way down the highway. I can remember our discussing the need to stop somewhere and add more water. The fish were becoming a black glob in the bottom of the tub.

If my memory hasn't failed me, I believe we stopped at the firehouse on Central Avenue, added fresh water and took a long break in the shade on the north side of the building.

We sat there leaning back against the building, dreading to get started again, knowing we had barely gone halfway.

It was probably Marvin who suggested we had rested long enough and had better get moving. He was always the responsible one. So, onward we trudged with our precious cargo, trying our best not to spill any more water. We knew that watering holes from this point on were few and far between.

We continued up Central Avenue for one more block, then cut across the open field at Fifth and Central and came out on Fourth. We continued east on Fourth and cut through some open lots and eventually came out on Chaffer

Avenue. After we passed the new Roxana High School, we sat down and took another long break.

The place where we were resting was the last shade available between there and Glendale Gardens because, after resting, it was our intention to go northeast, cutting across open fields all the way to Edwardsville Road.

As we crossed the open fields, we kept our eyes open for dewberry vines that normally grew there. Marvin and I had picked in these fields before and they had usually yielded a good crop.

Three hours later and about three miles from our origin, we finally arrived at our house in Glendale Gardens. We immediately filled the tub with fresh water, and picked out those fish that did not survive the long trip. Considering the temperature of the water by the time we got home, it was surprising that most of the fish were still living.

We were so tired by then, that we dreaded the thought of going on to Sones' Pond, which was probably another mile with half of it through the Vaughn's Woods. I believe we even discussed whether we should wait until the next day, but finally decided that the fish might not survive overnight. Those baby catfish had now become a cause, a purpose, a mission; we had invested too much of ourselves in them to take a chance.

I believe it was about six o'clock when we once again set out on the last leg of our journey and headed up Vaughn's Road as far as the viaduct, then cut through the woods to the pond. I suppose it was because we could see the end, that the tub no longer seemed so heavy.

As we crested the top of the levee, it was with a great feeling of relief and satisfaction that we viewed the water before us. We carried the tub to the north corner of the levee and set it down just a couple of feet from the water's edge.

We stood there for a few minutes before someone suggested we had better put the fish in the pond. Monty and I took the tub to the water and slowly started pouring the fish into the pond, watching the catfish swim in all directions as they hit the water. There were less than a half dozen that appeared lifeless on the surface when we had finished.

We stood rooted for some time, staring at the pond before we could tear ourselves away and start for home. We estimated that we might have put three hundred live baby catfish in Sones' Pond that day.

It was probably twenty-five years later, during one of my rare visits back to Wood River, that I asked Monty if he knew how our seeding project worked out, and he told me that Sones' Pond did become a very productive fishing hole. Whether it was due to our efforts or not, we'll never know.

*   *   *

It was only days later that we were back at Grassy Lake, only this time, we decided to hike on down to the canal and check it out.

To walk the banks of the canal and check out the debris left in the black willow thickets by high water was an exciting adventure. We would usually go all the way down to the spillway located approximately one-quarter mile from where it empties into the Mississippi River.

The Cahokia Diversion Channel is what we refer to as the canal. The Lewis and Clark historical site is now located at the mouth of this small river, although their campsite prior to their expedition of 1804 was located a few miles north at "Riviere Dubois" (Wood River).

The river was diverted some years later and now empties into the Mississippi a couple miles north of its original location, between the communities of East Alton and Alton, Illinois.

We gave little thought to the fact that we were walking in the footsteps of Lewis and Clark, while exploring along the canal that day.

While checking out the piles of driftwood and other debris, we came upon a wooden boat that had been deposited upon the bank and jammed between some willow trees by high water.

The boat was tipped up on its side and covered with mud and looked as if it was totally useless, but we had to check it out anyway. Because it was partially buried in sediment, it was quite a struggle to pull it free to a spot where we could give it a good examination.

Our excitement started mounting as we slowly cleaned the mud away and could find no damage. The big test, of course, was to get it into the water to make sure it was free of leaks. We slid it down the bank and slowly into the water. While holding it against the bank, we watched for water to start seeping in and, when it didn't, Tommy climbed in and sat down at the far end. Marvin and I quickly searched up and down the bank until we found two pieces of driftwood that would serve as paddles, and then hurried back. Marvin climbed in and sat on the middle seat while I pushed us free of the bank, then climbed in and sat down in the stern.

As we drifted into the middle of the canal, we anxiously watched for any seepage that might occur. After a few minutes of drifting, we knew we had a sound boat.

For the next hour or so, we paddled, mostly splashed, up and down the canal, feeling pride of ownership. We felt this was our boat by the same law that covered salvage rights on the open sea. Of course, we knew that somewhere up stream, in all probability it had broken loose from its moorings during a flash flood, and belonged to some fisherman or farmer – but "Finders Keepers…"

We continued to paddle the boat upstream to a position that was more accessible and closer to home. Luckily the current in the canal was usually very weak, except immediately after heavy rains.

While paddling, we were already making big plans for our boat. We even started discussing packing it with provisions and heading down the Mississippi River to New Orleans. This wasn't an impossibility, although at the time we never gave the slightest thought as to how we would return.

After we had hidden our boat in a safe spot and covered it with brush so others would not find it, we hurried back to Tommy's house. It was our intention to find some black and green paint in order to camouflage it.

Unable to find any green paint, we settled for a half empty can of black and an old crusty paintbrush, then headed back to the canal.

We once again pulled the boat up the bank and turned it over in order to finish washing away any remaining dried mud and let the hot August sun dry it before we painted it.

Our camouflage paint job did not turn out as we had envisioned. The brush was so old and hard that it was almost useless. We had to use it by daubing on the paint. After we had finished, we stepped back to admire our handy work and although no one admitted it, the hundreds of black polka dots made it look more conspicuous than before.

Although our attempts to camouflage may have failed, we were still proud of our boat and could hardly wait for it to dry. Every few minutes we would check to see if it was dry enough to be put back in the water. After about an hour had passed, we could wait no longer. We turned the boat upright and shoved it back into the water.

After being on the water but a few minutes, we noticed that the fresh paint was starting to wash away and streak along the sides, so we pulled it back into the hiding place we had chosen, and once again covered it with brush. We walked around looking at it from different angles to make sure it was not easily detectable by passers-by.

Tommy left us at the bottom of Velma Street and Marvin and I walked on back to Glendale Gardens. When we separated, it was our plan for Tommy to take the boards and do the paddle carving and we would meet the next day and take our boat on down to the Mississippi River.

During the long walk home, Marvin and I discussed all the equipment we would need for our trip to New Orleans. We knew of course, we would need lots of food (canned goods) that would keep, water, extra clothing, and some type of tarp to protect everything from the sun and rain. We never really thought about money. Of course, we were just exercising our right as young boys to dream and fantasize, without the troublesome need to question reality.

Marvin and I arose the next morning and, after eating breakfast, headed for South Roxana. The distance of approximately three miles one way was never in question. We would hike just about anywhere when the notion struck, with distance being of minor consequence.

We stopped at Tommy's house long enough to replenish our water supply and get his stuff together. Tommy picked up his bow and arrows and water jug, then the three of us headed for the canal. Our excitement began to increase as we approached nearer to where we had left our boat.

As we walked down the bank we suddenly froze – our boat was gone. We couldn't believe it. We stood there in shocked silence as we looked at the spot, now bare with the brush pulled aside, not wanting to believe we had lost our boat.

We quietly milled around for a few minutes, feeling sick and disappointed at the sudden turn of events. A day that had started with such high expectations of fun and adventure had suddenly turned sour.

Our shock and disappointment started turning to anger as we began to realize that our boat had not drifted away, but had been stolen. The water level had remained the same overnight, which meant that someone had to push the boat back in the water.

We reasoned that it could not have been the original owner because it had been stuck in the mud on the bank for quite a while and, if he had looked for it, he would have found it long ago. We were convinced someone had found it that morning and couldn't be too far away.

The culprits could have gone either direction, but we guessed they went down stream, and took off in that direction. The farther we went the more angry we became and the more determined we were to recover our boat. Tommy was really fuming. He had his bow with an arrow nocked and at the ready, and Marvin and I were starting to get a little worried that he might get carried away.

We were almost to the spillway when we spotted three boys paddling our boat down the canal. We ran as fast as we could and when we came abreast of them, we started shouting at them to bring our boat back.

The boys were about our age, maybe on the average a little older. It was obvious that they were caught by surprise and appeared shocked at our ferocity. We all three were screaming at them to return our boat. Tommy had his bow and arrow pointed at them, pulled to a full draw, when suddenly the stakes were raised. The older boy, who looked like what I always thought a thug to look like, raised his hand to show us that he was holding a revolver.

Needless to say, the look of that pistol brought our aggression to a sudden halt. We were stunned momentarily, and as we continued to demand that they return our boat, our voices had lowered considerably. We were still seething with anger, however, and were not about to give up on our boat so easily.

It was obvious that we had one advantage, they did not know how we had acquired the boat. For all they knew, we may have brought it from home, and we were not about to tell them differently.

As they started rowing to the opposite shore, we started running down to the railroad bridge about a hundred yards down stream to cross over. Our anger and indignation by now had returned to a point where we were not going to be buffaloed by this bully with a gun. We stopped just short of the bridge to devise a plan. Tommy was to swim across the canal and slip up the other bank, then cross over the levee and come up on them from the other side. Marvin and I would go on across the bridge and walk along the canal bank to where they were and confront them head on. Then while we distracted them, Tommy would come over the top of the levee and get the drop on them.

By the time Marvin and I reached the boys and the boat, two had gotten out and the third had taken the boat back to the middle of the canal and was trying to sink it.

As Marvin and I came running up, the thug with the pistol and the smaller boy had run to the top of the levee and were standing there watching Marvin and me. The largest of the three boys was standing with one foot on each gunwale, rocking the boat back and forth, trying hard to get it to fill with water.

While Marvin and I started walking up the levee, the thug opened the cylinder of the pistol, removed one bullet, and held it up for us to see. He knew we were ready to take him on and he wanted to make sure we knew the gun was loaded. At that point I don't think we really cared.

As we closed in on him, he put the bullet back in and closed the cylinder. Marvin and I had approached within about ten feet when all of a sudden

Tommy came running over the top of the levee with his bow fully drawn and aimed. The boy with the pistol, suddenly aware of Tommy, spun around and aimed the pistol directly at Tommy. Tommy came to a screeching halt about ten feet away with his bow still fully drawn. The thug stood with the pistol held in both hands pointed at Tommy – there they stood, facing each other – a Mexican Standoff. I was really afraid Tommy would shoot first, but after about ten seconds, which seemed like an eternity, the thug lowered his gun and yelled "Ah hell, give them their boat!" Tommy lowered his bow and everyone I'm sure sighed a big sigh of relief. I know I did.

The boy that had been trying unsuccessfully to sink our boat started paddling back to shore and got out. As he walked by us he was actually smiling and acted very friendly. As I've thought about this incident many times years later, realizing that someone could have been killed that day, I believe that we learned a lesson even though we didn't realize it at the time. There will be times in life when you have to stand up to bullies regardless of the odds.

We quickly reclaimed our possession and paddled to the other side of the canal, then went and retrieved our supplies.

Later, as we paddled down the canal, we were jubilant over our victory and the recovery of our boat, but at the same time a little shaken over the possibility of what could have happened. Years later, we all speculated on how long Tommy could have held his bow at full draw. Either Tommy would have had to shoot or lower it. On the one hand, if he lowered it, we would have lost our boat, or he would have had to shoot, and that would have been greater disaster. Perhaps the thug may have had the same thoughts.

We reached the spillway and struggled to get our boat over it. Water had not been running over for some time and the hot sun had dried the algae that normally made it so slick that you would be unable to stand up on it.

The slope of the spillway was at about a twenty-degree angle and twenty to twenty-five feet long. The hard part was to get the boat out of the water and over the top. After we had the boat past the flat area and onto the slope, it was much easier sliding it down the concrete to the water.

After we were afloat once again, we continued on to where the canal empties into the Mississippi River. The banks of the canal at this point were covered, for the most part, with trees and brush and lots of driftwood piled high in places. Looking straight ahead we could see the Mississippi, not more than a couple hundred yards ahead.

As we approached the mouth of the canal, a tugboat was passing by, pushing empty barges down the river. Tommy and I got all excited and wanted to continue on out in the river and ride the wake it created. Marvin, the more logical and responsible one, talked us out of it. After all, once we got out in the current we could very easily end up down the river five miles before we could get back to shore, and probably would never be able to return back up the river.

With the decision made not to ride the wake, we pulled onto a sandbar and started looking for a good hiding place for our boat. Because the terrain was very flat at this point on the river, we had to drag the boat for about one hundred yards across sand, logs, and drift wood. We worked very hard for about an hour to get the boat to a place we finally thought to be safe.

As we got ready to leave, we stood back and surveyed the area where the boat was hidden. We were satisfied that the only way anyone could know it was there, was by watching us hide it, and we were sure that didn't happen.

On our walk back to Tommy's house, we discussed our plans for the trip down the Mississippi to New Orleans. At this point in our planning, the thought that we couldn't do it never crossed our minds. After all, if Huckleberry Finn and Big Jim could do it in their unmanageable raft, surely we could do it in our rowboat. The fantasy itself was the excitement. Whether we would actually do it was something else entirely.

We separated that day vowing to get together in the near future and make our final plans. For days afterward we would continue to make preparations in our minds and occasionally talk about it. However, the day of embarkation never came.

Our procrastination and not making final preparations for departure was in all probability our fear of such an undertaking, although we would never have admitted that. A week or so later, we were provided with a perfect excuse – we lost our boat again – but this time it wasn't to theft.

It was shortly before school was to start that the three of us decided to go back down to the river and check on our boat. As we passed the spillway we started getting a little worried, because we could see that the water had been very high since we were last there. As we came to the spot where we hid the boat, nothing was left except a lot of new driftwood. The new high water mark on the black willow trees indicated that the water had been at least two feet over the top of our boat.

Our boat may have floated on down the river to New Orleans without us. More likely though, it ended up along the banks of the river somewhere downstream near Granite City. Hopefully, some other young boys with dreams of Tom and Huck found it and they too had their dreams.

Chapter XXIV

Fort Walnut

When school started in the fall, Monty and I were once again like Siamese Twins – where one would be the other would surely be close by. Each morning on the way to school we would meet somewhere along Central Avenue and continue on to school together.

Marvin and I would take as many short cuts as we could when walking to school. "The shortest distance between two points is a straight line" and believe me that is a fact that Marvin and I understood only too well. It wasn't long after school started that we had worn diagonal paths across every open field and wooded lot between Glendale Gardens and the Roxana school.

There was a wooded lot along 13th Street that we would pass through that contained a large number of brown tree lizards. These little creatures caused me nearly to be late for school on several occasions. I just couldn't resist the temptation to stop and try to catch them.

While walking through this wooded area one morning a devilish plan was beginning to take shape in my mind. In school that day I kept thinking about it. The more I thought about it, the more certain I was that I would do it.

I left for school the next morning about fifteen minutes earlier than usual. Marvin wanted to know why I was leaving earlier and I just told him I had something I had to do and took off running.

When I came to the wooded area, I started looking for the lizards, usually, especially in the afternoon when it was warm, they were everywhere. That morning I could hardly find any. Being reptiles and cold-blooded, they found the atmosphere too cool for them to be very active, something I hadn't anticipated. After searching for some time, I finally was able to collect five, which I put in a small paper lunch sack that I had brought for that purpose.

I hurried on to school and into my classroom with the sack folded at the top as if it were my lunch. The classroom was almost empty as I entered, for which I had planned. The couple of girls already there were milling around up front near the teacher's desk.

I nonchalantly walked to the rear of the room, opening the sack as I walked. When I reached the back wall, I slowly tilted the sack upside-down and quietly shook the lizards out on the floor as I continued walking around the room to the front, then on outside to the hallway, where I quickly folded the sack and put it in my pocket.

I was not anxious to go back in the room, expecting any moment to hear some girlish scream or other commotion that would indicate that the little varmints had been detected.

When Monty arrived, we stayed out in the hall as long as we could, as normal. We were never very anxious to go in and sit down. He was unaware of what I had done and I was not about to tell him or anyone until after the consequences of my foul deed was known. If it turned out very badly, I would not tell anyone. On the other hand, if it turned out to be a great prank, then I would tell Monty and Marvin and take the credit.

When the bell rang, I hung back as long as I could. While walking to my seat I glanced around the room and especially the back wall and windows, but saw nothing, and casually took my seat.

I sat there for the next couple of hours, expecting any moment to hear a sudden screech from some girl when she detected a lizard crawling up her leg – but nothing. The suspense was killing me. I couldn't concentrate on anything that was going on in the classroom.

When the bell rang for recess, I was one of the first out the door. I had to get outside, to move and breathe, to relieve the tension that had built up. I thought Monty could help me locate them when we returned to the classroom, but I wasn't sure I wanted to tell him before I knew the consequences of my little prank. In the end I decided not to tell him.

Nothing happened for the remainder of the morning. During the lunch hour I stayed in the room long after the others had left to make a thorough search of the room, but could find only one lizard trying to hide along the window frame near the ceiling.

My little stunt that caused me so much excitement and concern, turned out to be a big flop. No one ever knew those little creatures had ever been in the room. They were never seen again and to this day I don't know where they went. I always suspected they slipped out one of the open windows and escaped.

*   *   *

During the autumn and winter of 1942, war was raging all over the world. The scrap drive at school was still in full swing. We daily collected any type of metal we could find and took it to school. It would be weighed and we would receive so many war (savings) stamps according to the weight.

We learned on September 15, the Japanese had sunk the U.S. aircraft carrier Wasp, off the coast of Guadalcanal. In October, unknown to us at the time, the U.S. tested the XP-51 at Muroc Army Base in California, introducing the first U.S. jet aircraft.

On October 5th, the St. Louis Cardinals defeated the New York Yankees in seven games, to win the World Series.

In November, the British X Corp drove the Germans out of El Alamein, in North Africa and U.S. forces landed in North Africa, led by Dwight D. Eisenhower. On November 12, President Roosevelt lowered the draft age to 18 and, on November 15, the U.S. fleet defeated the Japanese task force off the coast of Guadalcanal.

German troops, after advancing within 15 miles of Stalingrad during the late summer, became stalled on the Eastern Front.

Except for minor diversions now and then, Monty and I continued to roam the countryside whenever we were free to do so. We still fished the ponds and creeks and hunted throughout Vaughn's Woods with our ever present BB guns.

Vaughn's Creek and Woods were not exclusively our domain. Lovers also found it a convenient place to spend time when they wanted to be alone. They used a short dirt road, about one hundred yards long that ran parallel to Vaughn's Road and the creek. They could pull off this dirt road into one of two parking areas that faced the creek.

Directly across the creek from these parking areas was a twenty-foot high bluff that ran along the creek at this point. On the top of the bluff heavy vegetation grew. This was mostly scrubby brush and trees, especially black walnut trees.

It was late one afternoon while Monty and I were walking along the top of this bluff that we came upon a car in one of the parking spots. We slowly moved away from the rim and worked our way to the edge directly across and above the lovers.

Most of our group, as well as Monty and me, had now arrived at the age of puberty. For some time now, we had been aware of the acts of procreation between the birds and bees – and humans. All our knowledge on the subject was acquired, of course, by the normal method – from each other.

Sex education in school was unthinkable in those days, and at the risk of offending today's education establishment, I believe they have erred badly. Their sex education programs have been counterproductive and have created more of the problem they had hoped to cure, but I believe they really knew that in the beginning…? I guess I still consider myself old fashioned. Society has apparently dealt successfully with sexual matters for thousands of years without structured sex education in school classrooms. I'm sure some educators will want to argue over exactly what "successfully" means.

As we lay there peeking over the edge, even though we couldn't see or hear, the thought of what they may have been doing was very titillating. We discussed taking one of the large green-hulled walnuts lying on the ground near us and lobbing it over onto the top of the car. We quickly rejected that idea because there was still too much daylight; we might have been seen.

The car soon left, but the idea of "Bushwhacking" did not. Bushwhacking is the noun we used to describe the act of spying on couples parked in lover's lane.

Monty and I, realizing what a great location we had, decided to build a small fort just over the crest of the bluff. We gathered several fallen logs and piled them about two feet high, giving us something to hide behind. We gathered walnuts and stacked them into small pyramids, like cannon balls, directly behind our makeshift parapet. Now all we had to do was come back after dark and wait.

We picked the next Saturday night as the best possible chance of catching lovers parked at our spot. Realizing that it would probably be after nine or ten o'clock before there would be any action, we planned to be there at about that time.

Because it was so dark that night, we crossed the creek near Glendale Gardens and walked along the edge of the woods through the soybean field until we came abreast of the position where our fort was located. Upon entering the woods we found it pitch black. Thankfully, the woods were only about fifty feet deep at this point and we were able to slowly feel our way to where our fort was located.

The night was cool but not to the point of being uncomfortable. We would watch through the trees at the flickering headlights of every car that came up Vaughn's Road. One of us was constantly saying "Hey! That one is going to turn in." Or, "Hey! That one is slowing down." We must have said that a hundred times before one actually did.

When the first car finally came in, it caught us completely by surprise. It came from the direction of Bethalto instead of Wood River. We hadn't been watching in that direction. The sudden flash of headlights sweeping through the woods caused us to drop quickly to the ground behind our barricade. As we peeked over the top we were disappointed, however, because the car pulled into the north parking area, which was about two hundred feet from our location.

After a couple of minutes our excitement subsided and we stood up and continued to wait. At one point we even contemplated going through the woods to the other spot, but decided not to, realizing it was too dark to try to maneuver our way over there.

The same obstacles that prevented us from getting there was also our defense. The darkness, the creek, and the bluff made it impossible for anyone to catch us, if they were foolish enough to try. We could slip away through the trees in seconds and be long gone across the soybean field before anyone could possible cross the creek and scale the bluff, even if they could see to do it.

We had been there for about an hour and a half and were starting to get discouraged. The night was becoming cooler and while standing around even with our jackets on, we were beginning to shiver.

It was somewhere between eleven o'clock and midnight when our victims finally arrived. As the headlights made their sweep through the woods, we dove for cover and peeked over the top as the car drove on past our area and slowed at the next.

Disappointed again, we stood up and watched the car continue on after seeing the other area was occupied. It pulled onto Vaughn's Road and headed back toward Wood River. We thought we had seen the last of that car, but it slowed and turned back in again and headed back to our location. We knew we had them then, they were ours!

Monty and I lay tight behind the logs for the longest time after they had turned off the car headlights. What seemed to us an eternity, we finally rose up and looked over the top. It was so dark that we couldn't make out the shape of the car, but we finally detected a dim gleam coming from the metal of the car's roof.

Monty and I had been very thorough in our preparations for this moment. We knew that it would be difficult to lob a walnut over onto the top of a car in the dark, so we had taken many practice shots during the day to get the feel of just how hard to throw and at what trajectory.

I suppose our nervousness is what caused out first volley to go astray. We each picked up one walnut and as we counted to three, lobbed them toward the car and immediately dropped down behind our parapet. We heard "thud, thud," as our walnuts hit the hard packed dirt of the parking area. We waited for the headlights to pop on, thinking they surely heard those thuds and would investigate. Nothing happened. We peeked over the rim of our fort and listened, but heard nothing nor could we detect movement.

After a few moments we were beginning to settle down some, the adrenalin had slowed and we were sure the next volley would hit the target. So once again we took up our walnuts and on the count of three, let them go…"Bong, Bong," two direct hits.

The sounds of those two walnuts hitting their target, reverberated through the woods like two small explosions. We weren't expecting it to be so loud. We froze in a fetal position behind our barricade. The lights came on and some squeaking of car springs could be heard as the startled occupants reacted to get the car started and out of there. The engine raced as it came to life and the wheels spun as it backed out and took off back toward Vaughn's Road. It hardly hesitated as it pulled out of lover's lane onto the pavement.

We stood up as the car pulled onto the road, then noticed that the car parked at the north spot was also leaving rather hurriedly. We were sure they had heard the commotion and were not about to stick around to find out what had happened.

Monty and I stuck around a while longer, but then began to wonder if they would report what had happened to the police. The longer we thought about it the more concerned we became and decided we had better hurry and get out of there.

While walking back home we figured they wouldn't report it depending, of course, upon their particular relationship and situation. We actually were concerned that we may have put dents in the top of the car. Monty and I were mischievous, but we would never purposely do something that was intentionally destructive.

We convinced ourselves that the metal was too thick for the walnuts to do any serious damage, and I now believe that to be true. The pre-World War II cars were definitely made of heavier gauge metal. It took quite a hit to put a dent in one.

That incident was about the total extent of our bushwhacking, although we would hear from time to time the experiences of others that had engaged in such activity.

Vaughn's Woods was not the only favorite spot for couples to park. The hard grassy taxiways or runways late at night were an ideal place to park. Wood River airport didn't have lighting and was closed after dark, therefore the chance of having an airplane land on top of you was virtually nil.

Chapter XXV

Hitchhiking to Olive Branch, Illinois

By late fall I had given up my paper route. The daily routine was just too demanding. Day in and day out, regardless of the weather, the deliveries had to be made. Decisions to become involved in other activities centered around the never-ending routine of walking to McCune's gas station to pick up my papers, then return to Glendale Gardens to make my rounds. I was too much of a free spirit to be tied down for too long, so I talked Marvin into taking over my route.

This did mean, of course, that I would not have coins to jingle in my pockets anymore. That knowing sound of coins clinking in my pocket always gave me a feeling of security. But that mattered little because Marvin and I always shared. When I had money, he had money, and vice versa.

With at least one of us bringing in a little cash, we still could afford to go once or twice a week to the new movie theater in Roxana. I believe the price of admission was a quarter. If we had fifty cents each, we could also afford a coke and either a box of popcorn or milkduds.

The weather was never a consideration in deciding whether to go to the movie or not; it was the movie itself that was the deciding factor. If the Roxana or Wood River theaters were showing a good war movie, we would walk through blizzards or torrential downpours to get there.

I remember our walking to the Wood River Theater one cold dark night during a severe ice storm. The freezing rain and sleet was blowing into our faces all the way, but not once did the thought of going back home cross our minds.

I can still remember the sound of the creaking and rattling of ice in the wind blown trees as we walked past the Brushy Grove School and the build-up of ice on the roads and sidewalks. By the time we arrived at the theater we could barely stand.

There were many times when the finale of the movie would be spoiled by the dread of knowing that in a few short minutes I would have to brave the harsh elements all the way home. Just as my feet and ankles were starting to warm up and dry out, it would be time to get out in it again.

On this particular night I was braced for the worst as Marvin and I left the theater, thinking that the ice would be so thick that we would probably not be able to stand, let alone walk all the way to Glendale Gardens, which was at least one and a half miles away.

As we walked through the side exit, we were met by a wave of warm air. The temperature had warmed considerably since we had entered a couple hours earlier and the sleet and ice had melted. Our walk home was uneventful except for a good soaking.

Our routine seldom varied when we would return from one of our nights out. We would shed our coats and head for the furnace register and stand until the chill was gone, then head for the kitchen. I, usually playing the part of chef, would start digging out the leftovers from the evening meal, or whatever I could find to make a snack. Marvin, who would generally stay on the register as long as he could, would call out, "Fix me one too, Ike!"

It may sound strange, but Marvin and I had now been given the nickname of Ike. We were distinguished by "Big" and "Little." I was known as little Ike and Marvin was big Ike, even though I was now larger than my older brother. Our cousin Veeda Worthington had come up with the nickname, although we can't remember the basis or significance of it.

*   *   *

The winter of 1942 slowly and drudgingly passed, but not without a major disaster on the home front. We learned on November 28th, that four hundred people were killed in a fire at the Coconut Grove nightclub in Boston.

With the coming of the New Year the war news was becoming more positive than negative. The Allies were starting to win more battles and were advancing on all fronts.

During 1943 the Germans announced they had discovered a mass grave in the Katyn Forest of Poland, where over 4,000 Polish officers had been massacred by the Soviets. This would later become a diplomatic thorn in the side of the USSR.

On May 8, American forces captured Bizerte, Tunisia. Later that month we captured Attu, in the Aleutian Islands. On July 19, five hundred Allied planes bombed Rome for the first time. On August 17, U.S. forces, commanded by General George S. Patton, entered Messina, Sicily, capturing over one hundred thousand Italian troops, and on September 8, Italy surrendered.

Although the most conversation around the dinner tables of Americans was centered on the war, other topics would divert our attention now and then. Baseball was still the favorite American sport and pastime, even though many of the star players had left to volunteer for military service. The New York Yankees beat the St. Louis Cardinals in five games on October 11, to win the 1943 World Series.

This year's Pulitzer Prize was won by Upton Sinclair for his work of fiction, "Dragon Teeth." The Jefferson Memorial was finally completed and dedicated on April 13.

Americans were now listening to the big bands, with Glenn Miller being one, if not the favorite. Radios across the country were tuned in to stations playing songs like: "All or Nothing at All," sung by Frank Sanatra; "I Couldn't Sleep a Week Last night," also by Frank Sinatra; "Sunday, Monday and Always," by Bing Crosby; and "I'll Get By."

Teenagers were now referred to as adolescents and had evolved into what merchandisers considered a cult, to be commercially catered to as never before. It was an age to be enjoyed and prolonged. No one will ever know why or just how this change occurred, but the war clearly played an important part. Young men below the age of eighteen were now the ones earning money from the many jobs available in the labor market.

Teenage girls were now earning money by taking babysitting jobs on a scale that had never been seen before. This was due to so many mothers now working in war plants – many working the night shifts. Parents were also taking advantage of this relatively cheap labor market and, with more discretionary money to spend, would spend more evenings out dancing and dining.

The first merchandisers to cash in on this teenage market were in the music industry, songwriters, publishers, distributors, and sellers of phonographic equipment. The next industries to recognize this teenage market were textiles, cosmetics, advertising, and magazines. Some publications were now solely devoted to the adolescent group, especially girls' magazines of fashion and makeup.

Girls were now starting to wear boys' clothes. With their baggy rolled up blue jeans and sloppy shirttails and with their black and white oxfords and bobby socks.

For teenage boys and young men, new faddish wearing apparel was forced on the scene by the fashion industry. Although it was not generally accepted in its radical stage, it did change the style of clothing young men would be wearing for the next few years. It was called the "Zoot Suit."

The headgear worn with the zoot suit was a rather flat-silhouetted hat with an extremely wide brim. The jacket had extra wide padded shoulders and tapered to a narrow waist, then extended to just below the knees.

The pants were high-waist and made to wear with wide suspenders. The legs were very wide and sloppy with large pleats and tapered at the cuffs. This outfit, if correctly worn, would have a large watch chain that looped down in front to the bottom of the jacket.

Only a few of the more fashion conscious, or brave enough, were seen wearing these radical outfits. However, we were all wearing pants that now had larger pleats and narrower waists and a tight fitting pants cuffs. These were called 'Pegged Pants." Some of the more progressive and groovy boys were wearing them so tight at the cuff, that they had to have zippers put in the bottom outside seams in order to get them over their feet.

Our sport jackets also reflected zoot suit styling. They had a little extra padding in the shoulders, tapered at the waist and were longer in length, but nowhere near the outlandishness of the zoot suit.

Now that Marvin and I were teenagers, we were starting to dress up more often and do the town. We would wear sport coats and ties, and yes, our pants were pegged and jackets tapered. The last thing we did before leaving the house was to make sure our hair was plastered down as flat as we could get it, using plenty of rose hair tonic to the point of saturation, At times it was over done. It was not unusual to see a light pink trickle, or drop of tonic running down the forehead of some teenage boy, including me.

Our routine was to start out for Reese's Drug Store if we were not going to the movie, then end up at Jive-Land (the Round House) for the Saturday night dance.

The Round House, was built as part of the original construction of Recreational Park in 1926, along with the swimming pool. Since then it has served several generations and is still doing so as of this writing, in what is now Central Park.

The Round House as well as the bandstand, was the center of our social activity. On many Sunday evenings we would gather in the park to listen to the orchestra playing at the bandstand. Quite often Ella Jean Paton, who was a neighbor living on Halloran Street, would sing solos.

On Saturday night we would gather at Jive-Land. "This was the happening."

"This was were it was at," to use jargon from the current crop of teenagers. Sometimes as you entered the doors, located on all sides except the west, you could hardly find room around the edges of the dance floor.

All the teenage boys, those our age, would cluster on the sides to watch and rarely dance. The floor would be filled with older couples and with a few from our group that were less bashful.

It was probably my third or fourth attendance before I finally got up enough nerve to ask a girl for a dance. I can't remember the girl's name or what she looked like, but I do remember the feel of her and the flushed emotions running through me. I can hardly remember ever touching a girl, let alone put my arms around one. I do remember hurrying from the dance floor after our clumsy shuffle was over. In my flustered state I failed to thank the girl, something that I never failed to do later on.

I returned to my group standing on the side. They all looked at me with smiles and grins of admiration as if I had accomplished some great feat and, in a sense, it was an accomplishment of sorts. I had forced myself to overcome my shyness.

After that first experience of holding a girl close, the intimacy of our bodies touching, was something I was determined to experience again.

Within a few weeks I was dancing every slow dance that was announced, if I could find a partner. Fast dances such as the jitterbug were not my style. Without air-conditioning, the dance floor could become sweltering. Those dancing the jitterbug would soon discard the jackets. Soon their collars would be open and their ties askew. They would be perspiring so heavily that their shirts would be plastered to their backs. This at least was the excuse I used for not dancing the jitterbug, but the real reason was that I was probably afraid that I'd make a fool of myself.

*   *   *

By May 1943 another move was about to take place. Real estate had now become a hot commodity. Housing was at a premium with values going up steadily. It had now become more profitable to sell houses than to rent them. This was basically because of the rent controls that had been put in place by the government.

If you were fortunate enough to have rented a house at a reasonable price, then the price was frozen for the duration of the war. Landlords could only raise your rent with your permission.

When the landlord of the property that we were renting, at 437 Harrison, in Glendale Gardens, approached Dad with this proposition, Dad flatly refused. This left the owner with no choice but to sell, which he eventually did.

It wasn't long before the Mayflower Moving Van was once again parked in front of our door. I believe by this time we were becoming one of their best customers. This was the seventh move we had made in thirteen years, and never more than three and one half miles away.

It was no easier leaving Glendale Gardens than it was all the other places that we had lived, but the house we were moving to was only about three blocks from where we had lived on Halloran, if you cut diagonally across the fields.

*   *   *

Reminiscing about the past, I sat there in front of the house at 437 Harrison for a few minutes; then started my car and drove away. I drove the same route the moving van had taken when we moved from Glendale Gardens in 1943. I went west on Harrison, then turned right on Edwardsville Road and continued until I came to Sixth Street, then turned left. After traveling for about one full block, I pulled up and parked just before Beech Avenue.

The house we moved to was located at 485 Sixth Street and faced west, looking directly up Beach Avenue. Marvin and I missed living in the country, but we were now centrally located and could easily walk anywhere in Wood River within a few minutes.

It was while living on Sixth Street that Marvin and I went to work at the Parkway Drive-in Restaurant located on the north side of Edwardsville Road at Wood River Avenue. The old building is gone now and in its place, at the time of this writing, is a Jack-In-The-Box, a fast food restaurant.

The Parkway was owned and operated by Mr. and Mrs. Purvis. I remember Mr. Purvis as a rather small man who appeared to have little to say about the operation of the business. I do remember, however, that Mrs. Purvis directed the operation like a First Sergeant. She was everywhere, barking out orders to the curb-hops, the cooks, the waitresses at the counter, and Mr. Purvis. I'm sure a business such as this required a firm and steady hand at the helm.

Marvin and I were curb-hops. As the cars came in and parked, we would run to the drivers' windows to take their orders, then run back to the window and drop off the order to be filled, and pick up any orders waiting to be delivered, all the time trying to keep track of which car ordered what?

The first few days on the job was confusing and nerve racking. I kept losing my customers. I would pick up an order at the window, then, forget which car had ordered it.

During the second night on the job, I carried around change from a five-dollar bill for about thirty minutes. I had lost track of the car whose driver had given it to me. At about the time I thought I may have the Grandaddy of all tips, Marvin came up to me and said "Hey! That guy over there is waiting on his change," pointing to a very irate young man sitting with his head sticking out the window, motioning to me. I ran over and handed him the change that I had already placed in a separate pocket and mumbled my apology.

I continued to work there for several more weeks until I started feeling tied down and restless again. I had other things I wanted to do and there just wasn't enough time off to do them. In fact, Monty and I had been talking for some time about hitchhiking to Southern Illinois. Our family had come from Olive Branch area originally, and we still had relatives there. Monty had relatives that lived in the Perks, Illinois, area.

It was on a Saturday afternoon when we finally made up our minds that we would do it. We were sitting on Monty's back porch steps and with little preparation and consideration to the time of day, I ran home to gather a few items of clothing and let Marvin know what Monty and I were going to do. I asked him not to tell Mom until that night; by then I thought we would probably already be in Olive Branch.

I hurriedly stuffed a pair of pants, a couple of shirts, socks, and underwear into a small gym bag, then slipped out of the house without Mom seeing me.

I met Monty at his house and we took off up Route 143 toward Edwardsville. We had no sooner gotten out on the hard road and stuck out our thumbs, when the first or second car stopped to pick us up. The man was going all the way to Edwardsville. We thought this hitchhiking was going to be a cinch. How little we knew...

The driver had let us out just short of Route 159, which would take us south as far as Red Bud, where we would pick up Route 3, which would take us all the way to Olive Branch.

We ended up walking the whole way through Edwardsville before we got another ride as far as Collinsville. From there we walked another couple miles through town. The next car that picked us up took us to the south side of Belleville. We continued walking until we came to a bridge just before leaving the city limits and resting for about thirty minutes. Of course, while there we just had to go down and check out the wildlife in the creek. After a few futile attempts to catch crawdads, we got back up on the road again and started thumbing.

We caught two more rides through the next two towns of Smithton and Hecker and finally arrived in Red Bud at about seven in the evening. We had been on the road for about five hours and had gone hardly one-quarter of the way.

The long summer days were in our favor but we were fast coming to the realization that we were not going to get there before dark. In fact, as it turned out, we didn't get there that night at all, and we spent most of it walking.

By eleven o'clock that night we were only as far as Chester. Every ride that we got was only going to the next town. With all these little towns about five to eight miles apart, we had usually walked about halfway before we were picked up.

The day had been exceptionally hot and we had been hoping that it would cool down after dark, but that didn't happen. It was a very hot night and the mosquitoes were swarming. As we walked by the Night Hawk Café on the south side of town, we were so thirsty we were spitting cotton balls.

For some reason that I can't remember, we wouldn't go in the café and ask for a drink of water. I've often thought about that. I never could understand why. But we eventually came to a house that had a sprinkler going in the front yard. We slipped up on it and pinched off the hose and took turns drinking from the sprinkler. We overdosed because we didn't know how long it would be before we would get another drink.

After leaving Chester, there were no more lights anywhere and the night was pitch black. Between the Night Hawk Café and the top of Chester hill, no cars passed us. We walked for the next couple of hours with only a few cars passing, but none would stop and pick us up.

While walking through the small community of Rockwood, only a few houses had dimmed night lights that shown through their windows.

It was now about two o'clock in the morning and we were very tired. We were stopping more often now and resting, but only for a few minutes. We couldn't stay in one place for long before every mosquito within a mile zeroed in on us. The constant swatting was adding to our exhaustion. We were sitting on the edge of the pavement at the crest of one of the many small rolling hills just south of Rockwood when we noticed a flashing of headlights through the trees above us. We jumped to our feet and got ready to start thumbing as soon as the car headlight came into view.

The first car that had passed us in hours went flying by without the slightest indication that he had any intentions of stopping. The car was about a hundred feet beyond us when the brake lights flashed back at us. We grabbed our belongings and ran to meet it.

The driver of the car was barely out of his teens and was going as far as Ware, Illinois, which was about another fifty miles down the road. Monty jumped in the front and I in the back. That was undoubtedly the most comfortable seat that I had ever sat upon.

We had barely gone a mile or so before I realized there was something missing – mosquitoes. Getting away from those incessantly annoying little monsters for a short while was a real pleasure indeed.

After a brief introduction and some small talk, we fell quiet. I had only been in the car about five minutes, when I suddenly became very sleepy. The steady hum of the automobile engine, the balmy wind blowing through the open window (no air conditioning in those days), no mosquitoes to fight, and a soft comfortable seat was more than I could withstand. It was a case of matter over mind. No matter how hard I tried, it didn't matter; I just couldn't keep my eyes open.

It seemed as if I'd just closed my eyes for a second when I awoke with a start. The car had come to a complete stop. We got out of the car stumbling around still half asleep, mumbling our thanks for the ride. As the young man drove away in the dark, we took stock of our surroundings and realized we were standing across the road from a church.

We stood there alongside the road for a few minutes, contemplating our next move, wondering if we should stay, hoping that another car would come by soon, or find someplace and hole up until daylight. We finally decided to go over to the church and sit on the front steps for a awhile and rest.

As it turned out, Monty had also gone to sleep in the car and both of us were still groggy. As exhausted as we were when we were picked up, twenty or thirty minutes of sleep was not enough to restore our energy.

We sat there for a few minutes, then stretched out on the rather large concrete porch to try to sleep until daylight. It didn't work, the mosquitoes found us again and started feasting. I was beginning to wonder how much more blood I had to give. I covered my head with another shirt but that didn't help, they were biting through the material. It was no use, I gave up and just sat there slapping.

As I sat there looking around, I noticed a large out building that turned out to be a privy, sitting off to the side of the church lot. Monty and I discussed the possibility of the mosquitoes being less of a problem if we could get higher above ground level. Well??

We decided to give it a try and walked over to the outhouse and found a large wooden box at the back that aided us in climbing up on the roof. The roof was slightly slanted and covered with tarpaper.

After about fifteen minutes of buzzing, slapping and scratching, we gave up and said the heck with it, and got back on the road and started walking.

By this time it was about four-thirty in the morning and we had been on the road for about sixteen hours and were still twenty-five miles from our destination. Normally the trip from Wood River to Olive Branch by car would take no more than three hours.

It was about five o'clock when we caught our next ride as far as the Cape Girardeau, Missouri turn-off. By the time we got out of the car, we could see light in the east.

We stayed at that intersection, deciding our chances to catch a ride with one of the early morning work commuters were better at that intersection.

Several cars passed us up before we caught a ride in a pickup truck. He asked us where we were going and I told him we were going to Olive Branch; he then asked if we lived there. I said, "No, we are going to see my Aunt violet." He asked, "Is that Violet Hausler?" I told him it was and he said "I know where they live, it's on the Brown place just before you get to town. I'll drop you off there."

I didn't know the gentleman and don't remember his name, but he obviously lived in the area because he knew my Aunt and Uncle Hausler, and also my Aunt and Uncle Bill Shockley.

He let us out of the truck at the bottom of the hill in front of Aunt Violet's house. As we walked up the hill to the house the sky in the east was a bright orange. It had taken us approximately twenty hours from the time we started until we arrived at our destination. Our expectation when we started had been to make it by dark...

We walked up on the porch and as I looked through the screen door I could see Aunt Violet and my cousins in the kitchen eating breakfast. When I knocked upon the door, they all jumped up and came running to the door. Aunt Violet came and opened the door and said, "Why, Gene Nelson, what are you doing here?" while looking over my head toward the yard to see if the rest of the family was with me. While she ushered us inside, I explained that we were alone and had hitchhiked by ourselves.

Monty and I were just as welcome at Aunt Violet's as if we were one of her own. She never met a stranger and her house was always open. All of the cousins within our families always felt as if they were home, no matter which house they were visiting at the time. I can remember my cousins saying that they always liked to go to Aunt Dorothy's (our house) because they always felt so welcome and there was always something to do.

Aunt Violet invited us to have a seat at the table as she started frying more eggs and ham. Monty and I stuffed ourselves. We hadn't eaten since we left home the afternoon before. I had to go back for seconds and thirds on the biscuits covered with sorghum and butter. Sorghum molasses must have been a breakfast staple during that period, because I remember it always being on the table, usually in a gallon bucket with a bail. That undoubtedly was one the most delicious breakfasts I've ever eaten.

As soon as we had rested some, I suggested we go into town; I was anxious to show Monty the big metropolis of Olive Branch. The first establishment we came to as we entered town was a little gas station and restaurant combination named "Twin Gables." Little did I know at the time what an important part this little restaurant would eventually play in my life? It was here, seven years hence, that I would meet the girl that I would eventually marry.

After crossing a creek we came to the blacksmith shop that was owned by my Uncle John. He had left for work by the time Monty and I had arrived at his house.

As we approached the shop we could hear the rhythmic ringing of the blacksmith's hammer, shaping white-hot iron on a steel anvil. As we came abreast of the shop, I could see Uncle John just inside the huge open door, in overalls and a large leather apron, pounding away at a piece of metal he was holding with a large pair of tongs.

Monty and I did leave home with a few dollars tucked away, but so far had been very stingy with it, but now I was anxious to take him to Slim's Place for a Cho-Cho bar, which was ice cream on a stick, covered with a malty chocolate topping.

Ransome "Slim" Ambler's store was a small place near the Methodist Church on Railroad Street. The building was long and not more than fifteen feet wide. When you entered, you would usually find Slim standing there on one leg, with the other knee slung over the counter. I always marveled at his ability to get into that contorted position. It always appeared to me as if he was standing behind the counter with someone else's leg lying on the counter in front of him.

Slim carried a small supply of assorted items such as tobacco, cigarettes, candy, some canned goods, soda pop, ice cream, and a small variety of lunchmeat sandwiches.

While Monty and I were sitting on the bench along the opposite wall facing the counter, eating our Cho-Cho bars and drinking Pepsi Colas, a huge John Deere tractor came chugging up and parked in front. The farmer jumped off and came in and ordered a Pepsi and dog sandwich.

A dog sandwich was a slice of Blue Bell bologna, about one-half inch thick, covered with mustard and placed between two foursquare saltine crackers. They were mighty tasty and satisfying. I would order them quite frequently in years to come.

We stuck around Slim's for a while, listening to Slim and his customers talk about every subject under the sun. Slim knew Dad. His two sons, Lloyd, who we called "Cat," and Max, ran around with Dad during their younger days while living in Olive Branch.

After we left Slim's place, we went to see another cousin, Billy Shockley. Billy was about a year younger than me. Marvin and I had spent several weeks the previous summer in Olive Branch, staying with Billy.

Billy wasn't at home, but Aunt Wilma told us he was over at the cattle barn helping Cecil Corner loading cattle in his truck. He was getting ready to take a load to the East St. Louis stockyard.

The barn was almost in their backyard and was where the Gowin Hardware Store is located at the time of this writing. Billy was there inside the barn chasing cows toward the loading ramp that led to the truck, while Cecil stood close and prodded them on inside.

When I popped my head over the fence and called to him, he looked up and just stared as if he couldn't believe what he was seeing, then yelled, "Where did you come from?"

After the loading was complete and the truck had pulled away, we bummed around together for the next couple of hours. By then Monty and I were both exhausted and headed back to Aunt Violet's to try and find somewhere to sack out. It had been a long hard thirty-six hours since we had slept, except for the twenty or thirty minutes in the car while hitchhiking.

When we got back to the house, Aunt Violet told us to go in the kids' room and lie down. I'm not sure, but I believe we slept through the remainder of the day and night, and did not wake up until breakfast time the next morning.

Monty left me the next day and went on to his relatives at Perks, Illinois. I stayed in Olive Branch and played with my cousins Willa Fern, Carol Lee, and Johnny. Billy also came over and we would play in the barn and run across the hills and woods behind the house. Billy and I also went fishing for sun perch in the creek that ran through Olive Branch.

Two days later Monty came walking up to the house. He had had his visit with his relatives and I got the impression that there were no young people his age to play with and he had gotten bored.

Monty, Billy, and I spent the next few days swimming in Blue Hole, fishing, walking up and down Black Creek, or exploring the bluff above the Silica Mill, just to see what we could see.

Aunt Violet and Aunt Wilma treated Monty and me just as if we were two of their kids. Never once did they give the slightest hint that we may have been a bother or nuisance. We came and went as we pleased without comment.

After about a week we decided it was time that we started thinking about returning home. However, neither of us were looking forward to another ordeal like the one we experienced coming down. We had made up our minds to start out hitchhiking before sunup and hoped for better luck.

We were at Billy's house the day before we had planned to head back home, when we noticed that Cecil Corner was loading up another load of cattle. When we walked over to watch, I suddenly got the idea to ask him if we could ride as far as East St. Louis with him. I was kind of reluctant to ask and asked Billy if he would ask for us. He did and Cecil said we could. This caught us by surprise because our belongings were at Aunt Violet's and it would take some time to go get them. When I told Cecil our problem, he said, "Go get them and I'll pick you up at the bottom of the hill on Route 3."

Monty and I took off running all the way back to the house and quickly gathered up our meager belongings while telling Aunt Violet that we were leaving and catching a ride with Cecil. We hurried down to the bottom of the hill and waited.

An hour later we were still waiting. As we sat there we were beginning to think that we had somehow missed him, or that he had decided to go without us, although I knew it was almost impossible for him to pass without our having seen him.

It was probably another hour and almost six o'clock in the evening when we finally spotted his truck coming around the curve in the road. We stood up and he came to a stop in front of us and we climbed up in the cab.

As I sat in the middle, I felt as if I was about a hundred feet above the road. I had never ridden in anything larger than a pickup, and was not used to being able to see so well. It didn't take me long to realize that the suspension systems were also not the same. We had gone barely ten miles before I was beginning to feel like I was being bounced to pieces. I realized then why Cecil was wearing a large wide leather kidney belt.

By the time we arrived at the turn off to East St. Louis stockyards, it was almost dark and my body was screaming to get out of that truck. I was never so glad to get my feet on solid ground in my life. My back was sore from rubbing up and down against the back of the seat. We thanked him for the ride and he asked, "Are you boys going to get home all right from here?" We assured him we would. It was just a matter of staying on Route 3, on into Wood River.

We were fortunate to get three or four short rides that put us in Wood River about midnight. We split up at Acton and Sixth Street. Monty continued on down Acton and I on up Sixth Street to my house.

Everyone was in bed when I walked in. We never locked our doors in those days, and I went on upstairs to Marvin and my bedroom and hurriedly undressed and crawled into bed. Marvin awoke and wanted to talk, but I was too tired. I told him I'd tell him all about it in the morning. I believe I was sound asleep within less than a minute.

Chapter XXVI

Runaways – To The Ozarks

Summer was always my favorite time of the year. Although autumn had its own kind of beauty and spring was always looked forward to with anticipation, it was the options of summer that kept me from ever being bored.

After Monty and I returned from our adventure in Southern Illinois, we were back exploring the wilds of Vaughn's and Ninth Street hill woods, or swimming at the pool, or in one of the ponds or creeks.

On Sunday mornings, Mom would still gather her brood and march us all off to church. We belonged to the Assembly of God Church located at the corner of First Street and Jennings, the only church we had attended since moving to Wood River. The Pleasant View General Baptist Church is now located at that location at the time of this writing.

Marvin and I, although teenagers, would still go to church and stay through Sunday school, but had an aversion to sitting through the Hellfire and Brimstone sermons. The preacher always looked like he was pointing or talking directly to me. By the time the sermon was over I just knew the Lord was going to strike me dead any minute for my sins of occasionally indulging in tobacco, or maybe going to the picture show.

Mom would always say as we would split up to go to our various classrooms, "Now boys, you stay for church!" We, of course, would never lie, we would just be noncommittal and usually not answer or pretend we never heard her.

Thank goodness for the basement exit. It served as our egress system. As soon as the Sunday school classes let out, Marvin and I would be out the door and halfway to Reece's Drug Store before "Bringing in The Sheaves" or "Rock of Ages" could be heard reverberating throughout the neighborhood.

I reflect back occasionally on the many years of sitting on those hard wooden church pews, and Mom's attempts at keeping her flock from fidgeting, fussing, and picking at each other. As we five kids sat, Mom would look down the row to see which one of us was causing the disturbance, then reach around behind and pinch a plug, as she called it, out of whoever was the guilty party. And no, it wasn't usually me.

I do know that those years did provide a spiritual and moral basis for many of life's decisions that I would have to make throughout the years that followed.

When Marvin and I would arrive at Reece's, we would usually take a booth halfway down on the right. If it was crowded, we would then take a stool at the counter; that way we would be waited on faster.

Our favorite order was either a banana split or a hound dog. The hound dog probably cost about twenty-five cents and a banana split, about thirty-five. The hound dog was probably my favorite. It was served in an ice-cream soda glass, with layers of hot fudge, vanilla ice cream, peanuts, and then a marshmallow topping.

There were times when we would leave church, and if we were real hungry, head straight for the Sunshine Coffee Shop for a hamburger. At least it may have been called that but actually it was a soybean burger. Soymeal burgers had become quite popular by 1943, since war-related meat rationing had created a need for a substitute mixture.

Marvin and I found the Soymeal burgers to be very tasty. The fried patties always had a flat brown crusty edge. When served on a bun with pickles, mustard, or relish, it was hard to tell that they were not pure hamburger.

I remember the Sunshine Coffee Shop as being a cheerful place, especially in the morning. It nestled diagonally on the northwest corner of Ferguson and Wood River Avenue. The morning sun would blare through the large windows, giving it a friendly and warm atmosphere.

Rarely if ever would we pass this intersection without seeing old Jess Whitmore either sitting or lying in one of the doorways, or hobbling along on his one rag-covered crutch. He was always talking to himself and, whenever a lady would pass by, He would loudly blurt out, "God bless you sister!"

When we were younger we were afraid of old Jess and would steer clear of him. When we would see him coming, we'd either cross the street or duck into the closest doorway to avoid him.

We always thought that Jess had been wounded during World War One; that he had been shell shocked and had his leg shot off. It was years later that we leaned that he was in the war but his affliction was due to accidents after he had returned. His mental state was the result of a severe blow on the head from a construction accident and later he lost his leg as a result of being hit by a car.

Jess was such a fixture and character of the Wood River scene that eventually a portrait of him was painted. I understand, although I've never seen it, that it now hangs on the wall in the First National Bank of Wood River.

*   *   *

A few weeks after Monty and I had returned from our Southern Illinois excursion, Marvin, Tommy, and I were planning another big trip. We were planning on running away to the Ozark Mountains. We were not running away from anything, or anyone, but we were running toward something – adventure.

We had long heard and read about the Ozark Mountains and wanted to see them for ourselves. We knew we couldn't tell our parents about our trip because they would never allow it, so we planned to slip away without letting them know.

It was a stroke of good fortune that made this possible. A couple of weeks earlier, Tommy and his mother were walking along Ferguson Avenue near where the Kroger Store was located when Tommy found a roll of money lying on the sidewalk. It amounted to twenty-one dollars.

Aunt Wave would not let Tommy spend it until they had determined that the owner could not be found. Aunt Wave had put it away, but Tommy found where she had hidden it. This was the bankroll we eventually used to finance our adventure.

Our planning sessions were much easier now because Tommy had moved to Wood River, just a few blocks away on Jennings. We would meet at his house or Marvin's and my attic bedroom on 6th Street. We planned our trip as if we were planning a military operation, leaving no detail to chance—or so we thought.

Each made lists of items we would need, then they were crosschecked and consolidated into one list. Our list contained one very important item, our ration books. Without them we wouldn't be able to purchase the necessary staples.

We planned in detail how we were to get our gear out of the house without being seen or anyone getting suspicious. We laid out the route we would travel on a map and we protected all this information as if it were a top military secret.

With our plans finalized and date set, all that was left, was to accumulate the items on our list just before we were scheduled to shove off.

The night before the big day, Marvin and I opened our upstairs bedroom window and lowered our gear to the ground by rope. After we had everything out, we casually walked down the stairs and outside, talking nonchalantly as we went. Once outside, we scrambled to pick up our gear and hurried to the garage and stowed it in a safe place until morning.

The one item that had to wait until the very last moment was our ration books. Early the next morning, I slipped to the drawer where Mom kept the books and thumbed through them until I found Marvin's and mine. Marvin and I then eased out the door before anyone else was up, left the house, collected our gear stowed the night before, and met Tommy at McCune's station, the predetermined spot.

At about seven o'clock in the morning the three of us with our gear, started hiking toward Edwardsville. It was a beautiful morning. The bright sun had just popped over the top of the hills ahead of us and was shinning directly into our eyes. The mild morning temperature was just right for T-shirts and overall pants. Blue jeans was a name that was rarely used by any of the boys in our group when referring to denim trousers. It was probably toward the end of the war when the term "blue jeans" became common.

We were in a festive mood when we walked away from Wood River that morning, full of energy and enthusiasm. We hurriedly walked along with a bounce in our step, turning and sticking out our thumbs at each passing car. No matter how much planning young people put into a project, they will invariably overlook the obvious, and of course we were no different. We were too optimistic with our expectation of catching rides. I should have known better, considering the experience that Monty and I had been through just a few weeks before. Many drivers will stop to pick up one or two hitchhikers, but are very reluctant to pick up three. Although we were able to catch rides, the size of our group put us behind schedule and caused us to walk farther than we had planned.

The first two rides we caught took us as far as Collinsville. From there we walked all the way through town. While walking by a small culvert we noticed a large cottonmouth snake coiled up in a clump of cattails. Suddenly this snake took priority over everything. We just had to get some sticks and pester it. However, by the time we could get close enough to poke at it, it slithered away among the cattails. With this diversion now passed, we gathered our gear and started walking again.

On the south side of Collinsville we caught a ride with a strange sort of fellow. He continued to quiz us about our hometown? After we told him that we lived in Wood River, he asked us all kinds of questions about the town. We finally realized he knew the answers but was checking our truthfulness.

He also had a very annoying habit while driving of accelerating then coasting, accelerating and coasting. Over and over he would do this to the point that it was driving me batty. This was the only ride that we caught that I was glad to see end. Marvin explained later that the driver probably had one of those freewheeling things that they put on cars to save gas, because at that time gas was rationed.

We were fortunate to catch a few more rides and by early afternoon we were on the south side of Bellville, Illinois. At the bridge just before leaving Belleville, the same spot where Monty and I had stopped, we stopped to rest and get something to eat. We entered a grocery store, located about one-half block before the bridge, and bought some bread, lunchmeat, cheese, and a small jar of mustard.

With our groceries and a Pepsi-Cola each, we headed for the bridge to find a place to sit and eat our sandwiches. We walked around and under the bridge and found a large flat rock that was ideal for resting. I can't remember and I've often wondered if we were required to relinquish any of our ration stamps for the lunchmeat.

After eating and napping for about an hour, we gathered our gear and headed back to the road and started hiking and thumbing our way south.

Somewhere south of Ruma, Illinois, we got a ride all the way to Chester. The driver of this car was dressed in khaki shirt and pants and Marvin asked him if he was a farmer. He said "No, I'm a pilot; I train army pilots." We have forgotten at what airfield he said that he was stationed, but he was a civilian, contracted by the government to train young pilots for the Army Air Corps.

By the time we arrived in Chester, Illinois, it was late evening and the sun was about to set. Just before the bridge that would take us over into Missouri, we stopped at a small Mom and Pop store that fronted on the sidewalk. The store was only about twenty feet wide and maybe as long. We bought a few items and of course, another bottle of Pop. The other thing I still remember buying there was a pink Snoball cupcake.

After we purchased our items we headed on down the hill to the bridge and walked on across. While at the middle of the bridge we stopped to watch a towboat that was chugging its way up river. It was moving slowly against the fast Mississippi current. We stayed until it passed directly beneath us. It was one of the older sternwheelers that would not be seen too much longer.

As I watched the boat pass below us I thought to myself what an exciting life it must be to travel up and down the Mississippi River. How little I knew at the time that within a couple of years I would be doing just that. I would also learn that the boat passing below was named either the Dorothy H., or Helen H., belonging to the Federal Barge Line.

By the time the boat was far enough away that we had lost interest, the sun had set. We knew we would have to hurry across and find a campsite before dark. It was our intention to camp overnight on the riverbank.

We had to go much farther than we had anticipated getting to a place where we could get off the bridge. By the time we could get off, we were a good half-mile from the river.

After we had worked our way back through the black willow thickets it was about dark. We quickly picked a spot that was almost directly across the river from Menard State Prison on the Illinois side.

Gathering as much firewood as we could, we immediately started our fire. After it was blazing brightly, we continued to gather enough firewood to last us throughout the night. This wasn't very difficult because of all the driftwood that had accumulated and settled around the base of the tree line.

It was after we had finished eating sandwiches from what was left of our lunchmeat and bread that we realized that we had neglected one other area of our planning – water. We shared the juice from a can of peaches but it wasn't enough to quench our thirsts.

After a couple of hours, sitting close to a hot fire to keep from being mosquito bitten, we were really getting thirsty. Finally one of us came up with the bright idea of boiling river water. We'd heard that boiling would kill any germs that might be present.

Tommy took the empty peach can to the river and returned, then placed it at the edge of the fire, and we waited. We were so thirsty by this time that we felt like drinking straight from the river. We didn't, of course, because we knew it could make us very sick.

We'd always heard the saying "A watched pot never boils" and now we believed it. It took forever for the water in the can to start boiling. After it did start, we didn't know how long it was supposed to boil.

After a couple minutes of staring at the can, we decided that no germ could live through that, so we removed the can from the fire and set it aside to cool.

For the next thirty minutes or so, we would occasionally pick it up and test it. Finally, although still very warm, it was cool enough to drink. We just couldn't wait any longer.

Tommy made the first test. He took a mouth full and kind of quivered as he swallowed, then passed it on to me. I took a big swig and almost gagged. It was the foulest tasting stuff I had ever drank. The boiling may have killed the germs, but did nothing to improve the flat stale muddy taste and we knew nothing at the time of the need to aerate water after it had been boiled.

Marvin took his turn and took several swallows. He really must have been thirsty. He also became sick at his stomach and complained about it for the rest of the night. None of us drank enough of the boiled water to quench our thirsts and we suffered throughout the night. It was about eight o'clock the next morning before we were able to find water.

The lack of water was not the only problem we had to endure that night. If we would back away from the fire, the mosquitoes would eat us up. When we curled up in our blankets and tried to sleep on the sandy ground, sand fleas or some other biting insects feasted upon us. What sleep we did get was very disturbed and fitful.

I believe that sometime during that night we all three arrived independently to the same conclusion and decision not to spend another night like this, and to go home.

By daylight we were already getting our gear together so we could hit the road as soon as it was light enough to get back through the black willow thickets without getting snake bit.

Before we left our campsite we definitely decided to head back toward home. After such a miserable night, our desire to go on down into the Ozarks and become apple pickers had faded as fast as dreams in daytime.

The first building we came to after we were back on the road was a small gas station and a few dwellings. We didn't know the name of the place at the time, but I now believe it was the community of Claryville.

I don't believe water had ever tasted so good as when we were finally able to drink our fill. We kept taking turns drinking from the spigot on the outside wall of the station, thinking we were never going to get enough. Just before shoving off from the station, we each had to take one more top-off swig.

We spent the whole morning walking, stopping at the St. Mary overlook to rest and look out over the Mississippi River and cornfields spread out below.

It was early afternoon before we walked through the town of St. Genevieve, Missouri. It was a very old and historical town, although we were not particularly interested in sightseeing at that moment. Our interest centered around food, drink, and rest, and not necessarily in that order. We had walked at least fifteen miles, maybe more, since leaving our campsite on the riverbank and we were getting awfully tired.

Having found a small restaurant and eaten our fill, we spent the next hour or so lounging around in a small park beside the road. It was about four o'clock before we seriously continued hitchhiking north and with as much luck as we had been having all day.

We came to a small fruit stand along the highway and bought a gallon jug of cider. It was Marvin's idea to get cherry;, I personally would have preferred apple, but I suppose I was outvoted. That was the way we made our decisions during the trip, democratically, by vote, and with an odd number there was never a chance for a tie.

During the next five hours we caught only one ride and had covered about thirty miles since we had left St. Genevieve. Almost half of that had been covered on foot and we were starting to worry about where we were going to spend the night.

Marvin was really getting tired and looking at any out of the way place to flop and stay until morning. He kept trying to talk Tommy and me into sleeping in the middle of a cornfield beside the road. Tommy and I were probably as tired as Marvin and didn't have any better ideas, but were not yet ready to give in and subject ourselves to another miserable night like the one before.

As we continued to trudge along in the darkness, grumbling and complaining about not being able to catch any rides, we soon came to a small settlement. As we got nearer we suddenly recognized a small neon sign that read "Tourist Cabins." Whoa! This was the answer. We could rent a cabin for the night. We still had most of Tommy's money. We'd been very frugal to this point and the way we were feeling at that moment, the only price that would have been too high would be more than we had.

Tommy and I were ready to run up and pound on the door but Marvin balked on us. He was worried that they would call the police. From the moment we had left home, we always avoided the state police. When we would see one coming, we would duck in the bushes. We suspected that our parents may have notified them that we had run away from home and they would be looking for us.

I think at this stage Tommy and I were beyond caring if we were picked up or not, but Marvin didn't like the idea; he was still set on sleeping in some cornfield. Again we settled the issue by vote and of course Marvin lost. Now the only question remaining was who would go up and ask for the cabin. There was some discussion as to which would be better, if one, two, or all three would go ask.

We settled it by deciding that all three would go to the door. When Tommy knocked, a lady opened the door and looked at us suspiciously while Tommy said that we would like to rent a cabin for the night. From what I remember, she appeared to be a little reluctant until Tommy told her that we had been hitchhiking back to Wood River, but couldn't get any rides and had been walking all day. She said the price was six dollars, probably thinking that would get rid of us, but when Tommy immediately peeled off the money, she was swayed.

The accommodations were definitely not Five-Star, in fact they would have been lucky to be rated a One-Star, but at the moment that didn't matter—to us it was perfect. It didn't matter that the only light was a twenty-five watt bulb in the ceiling, or that the tub was an antique, or that the water pipes growled every time the water was turned on, or when the toilet was flushed it took ten minutes before you could flush it again. None of these things mattered. We were clean again and we had beds with clean sheets to sleep on and only a half dozen mosquitoes were poised on the ceiling waiting to pounce. They could eat all they wanted, we'd never know it.

That was one of the shortest nights of my life. I closed my eyes and it was daylight, nine hours later. The older I've become the more I marvel at the recuperative powers of youth.

We left the cabin that morning feeling pretty good. We had rid ourselves of a half-inch crust of dirt that had accumulated from our sleeping on the riverbank the night before and we were wearing clean clothing. As we walked away, I realized that I had accomplished another first, staying in rented overnight accommodations.

I must mention here that most accommodations along the highways before the 1940s, were referred to as tourist inns, or cabins, or by some other title, but never motels.

Motels started appearing across the country after the war had ended, when Americans took to the highways in their new automobiles. "See The U.S.A in Your Chevrolet," was a popular commercial of the time, which helped, I'm sure, the proliferation of motels along the highways and byways of America.

Many dilapidated skeletons of these very early ten or fifteen-unit motels, that were poorly located or bypassed by super highways, can still be seen on many of the back roads of our country. Whenever I pass these long-forgotten and deserted symbols of someone's ambitions and dreams, it gives me a rather sad and melancholy feeling.

Fresh from a good night's sleep and a new plan, we headed toward St. Louis. That morning while getting dressed, we decided to go to the Highland Amusement Park and spend the day, then continue back to Wood River after we had spent all of the money remaining in Tommy's bankroll.

The bounce was back in our step as we headed up US 61 that morning. We knew where we were going and we couldn't wait to get there. We had been to the amusement park before and knew what to look forward to there.

From what we could calculate, we were somewhere near Festus, Missouri, when we were finally picked up by a man in a large truck. He said, "I'm going to the smoke, you boys going that far?" We didn't know where or what the smoke was, but we told him we were going to St. Louis. He replied, "That's the same place." We quickly jumped in and sure enough, as we drove toward St. Louis, I could see a heavy dark haze on the horizon ahead of us. That was the first and only time I ever heard St. Louis referred to as "The Smoke," and in those days it certainly was smoky. The buildings were black with sediment from the many coal-fueled furnaces that were used for heating during that period. I can still feel and taste that acrid burning in my throat from the coal smoke during the winter around Christmas time when we would go to St. Louis shopping.

The driver let us out downtown, within a couple of blocks of where we would catch the streetcar that would take us to the Highlands Amusement Park. We arrived at the Highlands about noon and the fun began.

With at least ten dollars left in the bankroll and rides costing a dime, we could ride to our hearts' content, which we did. In fact, Tommy and I stayed on the roller coaster four or five times without getting off. Marvin rode most of the rides, but he wouldn't ride the roller coaster.

We had our fill of cotton candy and ice cream and just about anything else we wanted that day. It was late evening when we stopped long enough to take stock. We were getting concerned that we would spend too much and would not have enough left for streetcar and Inter-Urban fare. The thought of having to hitchhike home from St. Louis because of our overindulgence was unthinkable.

It was dark when we left the park. The streetcar took us within a block of

172

the Illinois Terminal Street Car Station. These single car trolleys ran between St. Louis, Missouri and Alton, Illinois, making a stop at each community along the way.

I always remember this station as bustling with activity. Redcaps pushing carts of baggage along the tracks. People always busy hustling to someplace, but appearing never to get there. We sat there watching the activity for about twenty minutes before we boarded the car to Wood River.

The cars, from what I can remember, were about fifty or sixty feet long and rounded on both ends. They never turned around. The engineer could drive from either end and when it reached the final terminal, he would get out and lower the spring loaded electrical contact that was on the rear by rope and stow it under a hook. He would then go to the opposite end of the car and release that one from its stowed position and let it rise to make electrical contact. What had been the rear had now become the front.

After leaving the St. Louis station, it was only a minute or so before we were crossing the Mississippi River Bridge into East St. Louis. The electric car then stopped at each community from St. Louis to Alton. I remember stopping in East St. Louis, Venice, Granite City, Hartford, and it probably made other stops that I've forgotten.

It was pitch dark by the time we arrived at the Wood River Terminal. We had been gone exactly two and one-half days and we were really glad to be back home but we still had one big dread – walking in the house. We had absolutely no idea of what lay in store for us.

We walked across the tracks and headed up Ferguson Avenue, then turned north at Wood River Avenue as far as Penning. Marvin and I left Tommy in front of his house on Penning. We didn't wait around long enough to find out how he made out. At that moment we didn't really want to know; we had our own problems to worry about.

As Marvin and I neared our house, we sat down in one of the pits in the vacant lot adjacent to the south side of the house to determine our course of action. We were not more than one hundred feet from our house and we could see that the lights were on in the kitchen and dining room. The windows were open and we could hear voices, but were not close enough to determine what was being said.

Finally we moved on up to the house and crouched below the dining room window. The conversation was normal after-dinner talk, no concern for their wayward boys. No one appeared to be sad or despondent over our absence. If there had been any great concern, it obviously hadn't lasted very long.

Marvin and I didn't know what to make of it but we knew we couldn't stay out there forever. We had to go inside eventually and face the music.

We finally took a deep breath and said, "Let's go." We dropped our gear on the back porch and went into the kitchen. Mom was at the sink as we walked in and she just casually looked up and said, "Hi." We answered "Hi," and just looked at her. She continued to wash the dishes as if nothing had happened. We walked into the dining room where Dad was sitting at the table reading a paper. He looked up and said "Hi," then immediately returned to his paper. We could see Rita, Norma, and Jack through the archway in the living room. They too were appearing to act nonchalant about our return.

Marvin and I went on upstairs to our bedroom completely baffled by their attitude. We were also greatly relieved by our reception in a way, but still it appeared as if no one in the family gave a darn if we were gone or not.

It was sometime later in the evening after Marvin and I had gone back downstairs to find something to eat, that we were let in on their little secret.

While Marvin and I had been sitting in the field trying to decide what to do, they had heard Marvin cough and recognized it as his, and knew we were back home. While we sat out there they conspired to let on like nothing had happened when we would walk in.

It also turned out that Mom and Aunt Wave had gotten together and figured out what we had done. Although they didn't have the slightest idea of where we had gone, they knew we were off somewhere spending the twenty-one dollars that Aunt Wave had discovered missing. Uncle Tom said that he had the Illinois and Missouri State Police alerted, although Marvin and I were skeptical of his claim. We knew that several state police cars had passed us from both states and never gave us a second look.

Chapter XXVII

Greyhound Bus to Brookport

School started about two weeks after we returned from our Ozark adventure. This meant that Monty and I were separated once again. Our move to Sixth Street put me back into the Wood River school district.

School was a necessary aggravation that was tolerated because I had no choice. I just couldn't force myself to really try to get interested in the classroom, or other school activities, that is until I started the eighth grade at Lewis and Clark.

Actually it was my seventh and eighth grade. That may sound strange but I started in a program that allowed those students that failed the seventh grade to try and take both grades at once.

Yes, I failed the seventh grade during the preceding year at Roxana. I'm ashamed to admit it, but I must. For the sake of honesty, and accuracy, and considering my preoccupation with the outdoors, it was no doubt justified. Of course under the current school policies I'm sure I would have been advanced as long as I attended regularly, which I did with the exception of one day when Monty and I had played hooky during our fifth grade.

It was in the middle of March and we were starting to get antsy after being cooped up all winter. The "first day of March swimming tradition" had only sparked our desire, so we skipped school one morning and hitchhiked to the Alton, Illinois YMCA. That was the only swimming pool available that time of year.

It was about ten o'clock in the morning when we checked in. I was very uncomfortable, fearing any minute someone would ask why we weren't in school, but they didn't. Of course we didn't need bathing suits because they were not allowed. We were required to swim in the nude.

I'd wondered about that for years, until I did some research and found out that there were several reasons: first, in the beginning it was an all male thing; second, many of those attending did not have bathing suits; third, and probably the most practical reason, was the lack of adequate filtration systems.

Monty and I of course were unconcerned with those trivial matters at the time. We swam for several hours and left the YMCA at about one o'clock in the afternoon. Once back on the highway, we quickly caught a ride back to Wood River. Unfortunately school was still in session so we decided to find a safe place to lay low until school let out. We found a nice cozy spot in Fox's grove to hide until it was safe to be seen walking on the streets.

The next morning the teacher asked us why we were absent the day before and we both said we were sick. We knew she wasn't buying it, but she said nothing at the time.

By the second day I was starting to feel at ease and thought we had gotten away with it when the teacher came to my desk and said, "Gene, the principal wants to see you in his office."

My heart jumped up in my throat; I just knew I was going to get a paddling. Corporal punishment was the prescribed disciplinary punishment in those days and was administered on a fairly frequent basis.

To this point I had always avoided those infractions that called for such measures. The only time I'd ever had a hand laid on me was while squirting water from a drinking fountain in the boy's bathroom. The principal walked in behind me while I was trying to douse other boys. All of a sudden the seat of my pants exploded, and I scooted about five feet across the floor. In shock, I looked around just as the principal yelled, "You boys get out of here and back to your rooms." I was out the door before he had finished yelling.

On the way to the principal's office I wondered why Monty didn't have to come also. As I walked through the door the reason that I was called in alone was quite clear – there sat Mom.

I was shocked to see her there and it bothered me that she had been called in for this. On the way to the office I had already prepared myself for the inevitable – a spanking. Mom's unexpected presence unnerved me, and the brave front I was going to put on, disappeared.

I didn't get a paddling that day and I'm sure it was because Mom was there. However, if she could have been left out of it I would have gladly accepted a spanking, because the fifteen-minute lecture on truancy and wayward boys, given by the principal, was by far worse.

After promising that I wouldn't do it again, the matter was closed. I kept my promise and never played hooky again. The next time I decided to leave school it would be for a period much longer than a day: it would be for good.

It was while taking both the seventh and eighth grades that year that I finally got turned on to school, at least for a while. It was not because I had suddenly abandoned my Huckleberry ways, but because of one person, my teacher, Harriet Stevenson.

Even today, Miss Stevenson is the only teacher whose name I recall, or whose features I remember. None of the others made enough impression on me to remember them, except for Mr. Stahlheber, who lived across the street from us on Halloran Avenue and was the father of our friends, Jack, Benny, and Donald.

The reason I remember Miss Stevenson so well, I'm sure, is because she is the only teacher that made me feel like I was someone special, not just one of the herd, that I was capable of doing anything I set my mind to do. When she suggested that I take algebra that year I was hesitant but I had confidence in her and, if she thought I should, I did.

She kept me after school on several occasions, not for disciplinary reason, but to give me personal tutoring. I was not singled out for this treatment, I'm sure she did it for others as well.

That school year was the first that I accepted homework, although reluctantly. It was not only Miss Stevenson's influence, but also the knowledge that I couldn't possibly pass both years without forfeiting at least some of my free time.

I'd always considered homework a violation of my constitutional rights of "Separation of school and play." Later they were able to uphold a non-existing constitutional clause of "Separation of Church and State." Why not mine?

That year became doubly hard because, shortly after school started, I took on an after-school job. I had learned from a friend that Red, the proprietor of Red's Café, was looking for another dishwasher.

Red's Café was a small restaurant on the east side of Wood River Avenue about a one-half block north of Ferguson. It was about five o'clock in the evening when I entered the café. Although I had passed by many times, this was the first time I'd been inside.

I noticed the place was crowded as I worked my way to the rear. When I got to the end of the counter I had to stand because every stool was taken. I felt very self-conscious while standing there, while waiting for someone to ask what I wanted. I was being totally ignored as Red, his wife, and one waitress hurriedly went about their jobs. Red was cooking, his wife was handling the counter and their only waitress was waiting tables.

I moved aside once or twice as the waitress brushed past me, going and coming from behind the counter. I had just about made up my mind to ease back toward the door and leave as inconspicuously as possible when suddenly the batwing doors behind me flew open and out walked my friend, almost running into me. He stood there looking at me momentarily with a blank stare on his face, then blurted out, "Are you going to go to work?" I said "I don't know, I haven't talked with anyone yet."

He hurried behind the counter and started talking to Red. I couldn't hear what was being said, but Red turned and looked in my direction. He gave me a quick once over and said something to Bill, who immediately turned and came back to me and said "You're hired, now help me pick up these dirty dishes."

I hadn't been prepared to go to work that very evening and didn't know what to say, so I clumsily started helping Bill clear the tables and put the dirty dishes in the large pan he was carrying. When the pan was full I followed him back to the kitchen. Once there, he pointed to a shelf and said, "there are the aprons," then pointed to the sink and said "and there are the dishes." Although I knew he wasn't the boss, I did understand that as the new kid on the block, so to speak, I'd have to follow his lead until I learned the ropes.

From the amount of dishes I washed that night, I thought Red must be a millionaire. I later found out that first night was not the busiest night of the week.

I had been there about one hour when I thought my career as a dishwasher had come to an end. The waitress stuck her head in the door and hollered "We need some more dinner plates out here!" I hurriedly wiped my hands on my apron and picked up a large stack of plates and headed out front.

As I went through the door I tripped on a rise in the floor that I had yet to learn to avoid, and went sprawling into the dining room – plates crashing to the floor. One scooted across the floor like a hockey puck and ended up near the front entrance. With the reverberating crash of plates, there was total silence as everyone in the dining room jumped, and stared directly at me.

Confused and embarrassed, I immediately started picking up pieces of broken plates with my hands. When my hands were full I just stayed there on my knees, not knowing what to do next. It was then that my friend came through the kitchen door with a large pan and helped me pick up the mess. I believe there were two or three plates that were undamaged.

After we had cleaned up the mess and returned to the kitchen, I immediately started washing dishes again. I knew that at the end of the evening, Red was going to tell me that he didn't need my services any longer, or that he was going to dock my pay for what I'd broken. He didn't, and in fact, the incident was never mentioned.

I stayed with Red for several months and can't remember exactly when or why I decided to leave. The time I spent washing dishes for Red was the total extent of my dishwashing career.

It was during the Christmas vacation of 1943 that Marvin, Tommy, and I took a bus trip to our Grandfather Irey's farm at Brookport, Illinois. We didn't know it at the time but this would be the last adventure that the three cousins would ever have together again. It was only a matter of months before we would separate and each challenge life, with its many hazards and adventures, in our own individual ways.

It was very cold that morning in December 1943 when we boarded the Inter-Urban to go to St. Louis where we would catch the Greyhound bus to Brookport. In fact, that December turned out to be the coldest since 1935.

When Marvin and I left the house that morning, we walked against a blustering cold wind that occasionally spat snow and ice pellets in our faces. We took turns carrying the single suitcase that contained both our clothes. With our collars turned up and occasionally walking sideways or backwards to avoid the bitter wind, we finally arrived at Tommy's house on Penning Avenue.

The brief relief from the weather, if only for a couple of minutes while Tommy put on his coat and collected his things, was enough to thaw us out a little before continuing to the station. After arriving at the station, just across the tracks on west Ferguson Avenue, we only had to wait a few minutes before we boarded the Inter-Urban (Streetcar) for St. Louis.

Upon arriving in St. Louis, we walked the short distance from the terminal to the Greyhound bus station located on the west side of Broadway. I remember it as a huge large dark building, almost black, which could have been caused by coal smoke.

When we walked through the doors, we walked into a mass of humanity. The place was jammed shoulder to shoulder with people. We had not anticipated the holiday crowd, especially the hundreds of military personnel that had been given furlough during the Christmas holidays.

We worked our way through the crowd and finally got in line for one of the positions at the ticket counter. The line appeared not to move at all. It was probably thirty minutes later before we finally stood in front of a very harassed and frazzled looking ticket agent. One of us, I'm not sure who, told him we were about to miss our bus as he was stamping our tickets. For some reason that I didn't understand at the time, the statement must have annoyed him because he started stamping twice as hard, then shoved our tickets at us and said go get in line at the departure gate.

We squirmed our way through the crowd to the other side of the lobby only to find there were several departure gates with long lines at each. We finally located the right gate only to find that we were standing behind about fifty people all intending on boarding the same bus.

As we stood there we knew that the bus could not possibly hold all those wanting to board, plus we knew we weren't going to make it after discovering that all military personnel had priority; they were called to the front as each bus was called for boarding.

This may sound like a situation that would probably cause a riot today, but it didn't, not during that period in our nation's history. Not once do I recall hearing anyone complain because those soldiers and sailors were given preferential treatment.

Sure enough, we were bumped from the bus that we were expecting to catch. We stood aside as several last minute arriving military were called forward and boarded in our place. I can remember standing aside in awe as those soldiers brushed past us, some still showing the effects of combat. The only thing I can remember feeling was honor and respect.

It was about three or more hours before we finally boarded a bus for Brookport. Waiting those hours was really no problem for us boys. This was as exciting as anything we could possibly be doing, rubbing shoulders with soldiers and sailors of all different ranks and uniforms. We were aware of what the many campaign ribbons represented. We saw many that were on crutches, some with a leg or arm missing; others with their faces bandaged, covering disfiguring wounds. The sights we saw that day have forever been etched in our minds.

The bus trip to Brookport, which is located just across the Ohio River from Paducah, Kentucky, took about five hours and was uneventful except for the dozen or more stops made along the route. There was very little conversation as the bus traveled across the cold colorless countryside of Southern Illinois, made to look more sober by the gray overcast day.

During the spring and summers these empty dead frozen fields would be alive with waves of winter wheat or row upon row of tall stalks of corn. The cottonwood and soft maple trees that lined the ditches along the way would be lush and green with foliage.

At times the bus would make stops at small communities to drop off one or two passengers and sometimes pick up a few. Each time we would be greeted by a draft of cold air through the bus door that would be left open briefly

It was the stops at larger towns that had bus stations with cafes and restrooms that I always looked forward to, because I would have invariably consumed more beverage than I should have at the last stop, and would be sitting there in misery with my legs crossed by the time we arrived at the next station. Buses were not equipped with lavatories in the 1940s.

Those stops also gave us a chance to stretch and rest our tailbones. The suspension systems and seats on those buses were not as good as the ones of today and the short rests were very welcomed.

It was late evening when we arrived and Grandpa was there to meet us when the bus pulled into the station. By the time we arrived at the farm, which was about one mile east of town, it was almost dark.

Grandma had a big supper ready on the table when we arrived. I always remember each meal at Grandma Irey's as being a lavish spread. There always appeared to be more food on the table than my plate would hold and I usually filled up before I could try everything. She always had large loaves of home-baked light bread served with real home-churned butter and jars of jellies and jams. This was washed down with all the fresh milk you wanted and of course desert; usually pie or cake and sometimes both. In the summer there would be all the strawberry shortcake you wanted that was made in a dishpan. For some reason everyone thought that made it taste better.

That evening after supper, our cousins came out to the farm and we all sat around the dining room table with a big pan of popcorn and listened to Grandpa tell wild stories.

It was very cold that night and when we finally retired for the night, that big feather bed really felt warm and snugly. Marvin and I slept together and we can't remember where Tommy slept.

The next day we wandered around the farm and climbed in the barn and the hayloft and helped Grandpa feed the livestock. When it became milking time, Grandpa put Marvin to work. Marvin just happened to be the only one of us boys that knew how to milk a cow. A couple of summers earlier he had spent his summer vacation on the farm and Grandpa had taught him how and that had become one of his daily chores while staying there.

The day before we were to return home, we went into Brookport shopping with Grandpa. His grocery list was usually very short because the farm was almost self-sufficient. They would usually contain such items as flour, sugar, coffee, baking powder, cheese, and a few other essential staples. Corn Flakes breakfast cereal was probably his only extravagance.

Grandpa parked his car near the water tower, approximately one-half block east of the Kroger store, where he usually shopped. As Grandpa went about his business of getting his order filled, we boys milled around and waited for him. It was while Grandpa was ordering a pound of round longhorn cheese that I recalled a trick he had played on Marvin and me a few years earlier while we were visiting him. Marvin and I had also accompanied him to the store on that occasion and, while there, he asked us what kind of cheese we liked. We told him that we liked square cheese, meaning American brick cheese.

That evening as Marvin and I sat down at the dining room table preparing to eat, Grandpa came out of the kitchen carrying a plate of longhorn cheese except that it had been altered—he had trimmed off the round edges. He sat it down before us saying. "There's your square cheese you guys like so much." Grandpa was quite the prankster; he was full of little stunts like that.

We stayed with our cousins, Veeda and Bobby, the night before we were to leave for home. We cousins always enjoyed being with each other, and since they had moved away from Wood River a few years earlier, we rarely got to visit.

Staying overnight at their house gave us ample opportunity to get our talking out. Marvin didn't tell any of his long captivating tales that we all used to enjoy so much this time, he had outgrown that by now.

The next morning as we walked the few blocks to a gas station, located at the foot of the Ohio River Bridge, a cold freezing rain was falling. A thin glaze of ice was already starting to form on the limbs of the bare trees as we waited for the bus.

Although we were sheltered from the slow freezing drizzle, our toes were starting to get a little nipped by the time the bus popped over the high point of the bridge and came pulling into the station.

When the door opened a couple of people got off, as well as the driver who opened the baggage compartment to retrieve their luggage and toss ours in. After he closed the compartment, he climbed back aboard and we followed. As he collected our tickets I looked around and could clearly see that the bus was full with a couple of people standing. As the bus pulled out of Brookport, we three were also standing in the aisle holding to the overhead baggage rails.

I glanced around the bus seeing that there were three Air Corps Sergeants on board. Two of them were Technical Sergeants (five stripes) and the third was a Staff Sergeant (four stripes.)

We remained standing for the next hour or so, before there were seats available for us to sit. By the time we had been on the bus for about two hours, the weather had worsened and now the road was starting to become extremely icy. It was shortly after that that almost all traffic had come to a standstill. Our bus was about the only vehicle still on the highway and we were creeping along at about ten miles per hour. We were concerned that at any minute we would start sliding over the shoulder and into the roadside ditch.

After what seemed an eternity of creeping along, the bus driver slowly pulled off the road and stopped in a parking lot of a large barn-like building that turned out to be a restaurant. This would have normally been our next stop anyway, however, this rest stop turned out to last for the next twenty-two hours.

That ice storm continued all through the day and well into the night. By the time the freezing rain had stopped, there was about an inch of ice covering everything, including the highways.

While sitting in the bus, we could look out of the windows and watch the progress of the icicles lengthening as the night wore on. The driver kept the bus engine running and the heaters going, plus we could go back and forth from the restaurant to the bus as the need arose.

We would occasionally go inside and get a cup of hot coffee, or something to eat, but most of the time spent on the bus was trying to find a comfortable position that would allow periods of catnapping. There were many muffled and hushed conversations going on throughout the bus. It was during these long restless hours that we learned the story of the three Army Air Corps Sergeants.

They had been rather quiet most of the time and I had noticed earlier that they really didn't seem to have much to say, even among themselves. They appeared to be very introspective, deep in their own thoughts.

It was only through bits of conversation throughout the night that we learned they were B-17 bomber crewmembers, who had just arrived stateside after completion of their required twenty-five bombing raid missions over Germany.

During the early days of daylight bombing, a third to one-half of the bombers were being shot out of the sky. These men had to sit there, mission after mission, watching their comrades being killed all around them, knowing that with each mission the odds were against them making it through to the twenty-fifth mission. The emotional strain of such an ordeal had to be debilitating, especially after having experienced it so recently. It's easy to see now why their demeanor was so quiet and reflective. I've often wondered if any or all were carrying letters or messages to a wife or mother of a buddy who had been lost.

When the driver finally announced we were going to leave, it was with jubilation that we all scrambled to get back aboard. I had become comfortable with the place, the employees, and the camaraderie. Later we determined that the place where we had been stranded overnight was the small community of Ashley, Illinois, known as the Ashley "Y."

The remainder of the trip across the flat Southern Illinois countryside, except for slight undulations, was uneventful, and within a couple of hours, we were pulling into the St. Louis station.

As we stepped from the bus everyone kind of hesitated and looked around at each other, smiled or waved and said something ridiculous like, "Take it easy," or "See ya," then turning with each person going their own way, knowing that circumstances brought them together for a brief time in their lives, only to go their own way—never to meet again.

The three of us transferred to the Inter Urban and by the time we arrived in Wood River, all evidence of the ice storm had disappeared. The walk home from the station, although cool, damp, and gloomy, was considerably different from the frigid weather of the day we left. But that is the norm and to be expected during Midwestern winters.

Chapter XXVIII

The War Claims A Friend

Except for occasionally meeting soldiers or sailors around town and seeing some of our friends a couple of years older being drafted or enlisting, the war for us was an abstract thing. We listened to the news and kept abreast of the large battles that we would win or lose, but we were nevertheless unaffected by it. That is, until the first week of January 1944.

It was only about ten days or so after we had returned from our trip to Brookport, Illinois, that we got the news that one of our boyhood friends had been killed in action.

Marvin and I were just leaving the house when we spotted Benny and Donald Stahlheber coming across the field toward us. We met them in the middle of the field and as we met, Benny said, " Didn't you guys have a friend in South Roxana named Charles McDonough?" When we told him we did, he then said, "It was in the paper that he's been killed in the South Pacific."

We stood there momentarily in shocked silence, while the news of what we had just been told sank in. Marvin then asked, "Are you sure?" Benny responded by reaching into his pocket, pulling out the newspaper clipping and handed it to Marvin.

Even after reading it, it was still hard to believe that someone we had played with almost on a daily basis could possibly have been killed in the war.

Charles (Cherb) McDonough, was a year older than Marvin, but had lied about his age, as so many had done to join the Marines. All of us teenage boys would have done the same if we thought we looked old enough to pull it off. It was the patriotic thing to do as well as the lure of excitement and the glamour of the uniform. The thought of getting killed of course was never a consideration; that is something that happens to someone else.

We later were told that Cherb had been killed during the invasion of Cape

Gloucester Bay on the island of New Britain. It was hard to believe that one of our gang had died on some unheard-of island in the South Pacific, almost seven thousand miles from our playgrounds of South Roxana. Those little banners with their gold stars suddenly had a real meaning; we now looked upon them with reflection and a new Understanding. Before the war was over, many young men that we knew and had played with, or were acquainted with would become directly involved in the war. Arthur Roos, one of our friends who lived down the street from us when we lived on Halloran, became a prisoner of war in Germany. Russell Dunham of Brighton, The brother of Mrs. Jack Ritter of Wood River, won the Congressional Medal of Honor for his heroic feats in the Alsacian section of the Western Front. Robert E. Ryan was awarded the Distinguished Flying Cross for his action while flying the "Hump" in the India-China Theater. Many more, whose names I can't recall, would be mentioned in the newspapers before the war was over.

1944 was definitely the turning point of the war. Allied forces were expanding operations and advancing on all fronts. Before the year was over, we had recovered most of the territories lost earlier to the Japanese.

U. S. forces recaptured the Islands of Guam, Saipan, and Tinian – where napalm, a highly incendiary jelly-like substance used in bombs and flame-throwers was used for the first time.

The Japanese lost over four hundred planes and three aircraft carriers by the time the battle of the Philippines Sea ended in late June.

Our forces invaded the island of New Guinea and General MacArthur kept his promise and returned to the Philippines on October 20, as his forces landed at Leyte. On October 26, the battle of Leyte Gulf ended with the defeat of the Japanese forces. That turned out to be the largest naval battle of World War II.

In the European theater of operations, the allied forces entered Rome on May 18, and the Normandy Invasion began on June 6, with over four thousand ships of various kinds eventually landing four million allied troops on the beaches of Normandy in France.

The Germans introduced a new weapon of war against England on July 13, the V-1 rocket. By August, Brittany had fallen to the Allies and the drive toward Paris was on, and on August 25, Paris was liberated from the German occupiers.

In December the Germans launched their last big push. The Battle of the Bulge started on the 16th, as the Germans forces broke through the allied lines in the Ardennes. During the Battle of the Bulge, the famous reply "NUTS," was given by General McAuliffe to the German demand to surrender his forces in the Ardennes.

*   *   *

We had been living on Sixth Street barely nine months when we got the news that we were to move once more. Our landlord, who had been a bachelor, decided to get married and wanted the house for he and his new bride. This meant that Mom and Dad had to scramble to find another place for us to live.

Housing was becoming extremely hard to find and I'm not sure what we would have done if it weren't for the Defense housing in East Alton. Because Dad's job at the Shell Oil Refinery was classified as defense work, we were entitled to one of these units located at the north end of Whitelaw Street.

When I first got the news that we were moving I was really worried because of my school situation. I was afraid that I would have to transfer to the East Alton district and that would have created a real problem for me. As it turned out, they allowed me to finish the school year where I was because only a couple of months remained in the school year.

Although we had lived on Sixth Street a relatively short time, it was still hard to leave. We were so centrally located to all of our areas of interest such as the woods, downtown Wood River, the Round House and swimming pool area, the gang on Halloran, and the schools.

By the time the Mayflower moving van parked in front of our house again, the excitement of the moving and experiencing something new lessened our disappointment at leaving Sixth Street. I'm sure by now Mom and Dad were regretting selling the house on Leslie, or these last three moves would never have been necessary. For us kids, of course, each move was a wealth of adventure that otherwise we would never have experienced.

*   *   *

I sat in my car looking across the street at the house at 485 Sixth Street, trying to remember the particulars of that move in 1944, with no success. I'm sure we must have moved on a weekend or I would have remembered leaving one house in the morning and returning to another after school in the evening.

While sitting there contemplating my next move I looked at my watch and realized it was past lunch time and I was starting to feel it, so I started the car and drove south and turned left on Halloran and drove back to the Pancake Ranch.

When I walked in I recognized a couple of the waitresses who were still there from breakfast. As I glanced around the room, it appeared as if no one had left; they looked very similar to the morning crowd. One older gentlemen sat at a table with a couple of others about my age. He was wearing a green ball cap with white letters that told everyone that he was a "Crabby Old Fart." If it offended anyone, there was no indication.

I sat there eating my cheeseburger and fries and watched the crowd come and go, thinking about how my life had changed since living here so many years ago. A gentleman walked in and sat down and for some unexplainable reason caused a flashback to an incident that occurred while living on Halloran during 1941.

We boys were always pulling some kind of prank on each other. On this particular day it was Bobby Ritter's turn. There were about five or six boys that had gathered in our front yard, when Marvin stepped up to Bobby and started looking behind his ear. When Bobby jerked away, Marvin said very seriously, "Hey Bobby, let me look at that." We all gathered around and silently looked behind Bobby's ear, then one of us said, "Yeah, that's it." Bobby jerked away again and with alarm yelled, "What is it?" "What is it?" We didn't answer him but looked at each other, shaking our heads and in unison solemnly said to each other, "Yes, that's it."

Bobby, with his eyes big and feeling behind his ear, asked again what was wrong. Marvin stepped up one more time and took another good look behind his ear, then looked him straight in the eye and said, "Bob, you've got Blue-Goofous, the first stages of Yellow-Coccanous, and it's deadly." Bobby, who was about seven or eight years old at the time, turned and took off for home as fast as he could go.

Our laughter and fun at Bobby's expense lasted only about as long as it took for him to tell his mother that he was about to die, when suddenly, their door opened and out came Mrs. Ritter pulling Bobby along behind, heading for our house. We took off for the back yard as she came across the street and marched up on our front porch and rather forcefully knocked at the door. Of course we were no longer in hearing range, but later learned that she told Mom in no uncertain terms that the only thing wrong with Bobby was a rash, a revelation of which we were totally unaware.

I sat there nursing my coffee, thinking about my next stop and what I might find when I got there. I decided it was time to get moving so I gulped down the last of my third refill, paid my bill and left the restaurant.

I pulled out on the highway and headed west until I came to Whitelaw, then turned right. As I approached the end I slowed and looked for the number 420. It was on the right so I went to the end of the street and turned around and came back and parked where I could look at the front door.

There were two units to each building. The one in which we lived in, 420, was on the west end, next to Whitelaw. In 1944, there was a street lamp just across the street above a telephone booth. This was the congregating point for all the kids in the immediate vicinity. On any given night you would find anywhere from two to ten kids playing there.

It may be interesting to note that the telephone booth was the only telephone in the area. To my knowledge, none of the units had private phones. Also to my knowledge the booth and telephone were never vandalized while we lived there. This may very well be a good example of the difference in the level of hooliganism compared to the present.

As I glanced around at the buildings, I noticed that they looked a little worse for wear. Some, of course, were well kept and others appeared run down. They had been almost new when we moved here. It didn't take long for us kids to get acquainted with the kids in the neighborhood.

In 1944, there was only farmland north of St. Reed Drive. Douglas Avenue never excited, only a sidewalk that ran north and south along the entire length of the east side of the housing complex. Across the sidewalk, where Douglas Avenue is now located, was open farmland and fields that ran all the way to the bottom of the hill. This field was split by a drainage gully that ran diagonally across it from northwest to southeast. Beyond the gully was sage grass and scrub brush that ran up over the hill. At the top of the hill stood a large lone oak tree and just beyond that was woods that ran all the way through to Ninth Street.

This same open field is where we played ball and flew our kites. Just beyond the drainage gully all the way to Ninth Street is where we hunted rabbits and squirrels. During one of our hunts, Monty shot a pheasant while we were hunting in the fall of 1944, just across this gully, probably where Amherst Drive is located today. We were very surprised because pheasants were rarely seen that far south in Illinois. They usually stayed north of the lime belt that ran north of the Wood River and Alton area.

Kite flying was a big thing with us kids. Most of the time we would make our own out of whatever material we could scrape together. The cross-sticks were the major problem and were the hardest to find. We would split the slats of orange crates whenever we could find them. It usually took a lot of whittling and shaving to get them thin enough to use.

With the sticks tied as a cross, one slightly shorter than the other, a string was then run all the way around from tip to tip. This frame was then covered with newspaper, attached with flour paste. The tail was made from strips of rags. The velocity of the wind determined the length of the tail. On relatively calm days, very little tail would be needed. On windy days a longer tail would have to be added.

It was the addition of the parachute that added so much to the fun of kite flying. Just standing there holding a ball of twine could become boring after a couple of hours, but lost in the experimentation with various kinds of parachutes, we could spend a whole day flying kites.

We found that the best parachutes were made from the tissue wrappings that came with Sunkissed Oranges. The tissue was very light and bright orange, which made it highly visible. By tying a ten-inch long string to each corner then bringing them together at the bottom where a toy lead soldier or a small nut or bolt provided ballast, we had a perfect parachute. We would use the parachutes by "running down the line'" as we called it. With the kite airborne, one of us would tuck the string under our arm and run toward the kite until we were about halfway, then attach the parachute to the kite string by a shallow hook attached at the middle of the parachute material. When the string was released, the wind would push the chute up the string toward the kite. The key to a good release was in the timing; it had to be just a few feet before reaching the kite for the best results.

Flipping a loop in the string, which would jar the chute loose, made the release. If you failed to do this before the chute reached the kite, it was then almost impossible to shake it loose. When this occurred, it was necessary to once again run down the string and bring it back halfway and try again.

Whether it was kite-flying, ball playing, or just hanging out under the street lamp with our new friends, we soon felt very much at home living in the defense houses, as they were known by the local vernacular.

I continued to concentrate on school for the remainder of the school year. There were about two weeks left in the school year when Miss Stevenson asked me to stay after school for a few minutes, that she wanted to talk to me. I wasn't sure what to expect, but when she informed me that I would be graduating, I let out a big sigh of relief. I had really been worrying about it for sometime and couldn't imagine not going on to high school with the rest of my friends. I had attended school with that same group ever since the third grade, with the exception of the previous year.

I was also reaching an age where my ego and pride was starting to influence my actions. I was beyond the age of childish self-gratification above all else. Image had now become important.

Our eighth grade graduation ceremony that year was held in the Wood River High School gymnasium. We were required to wear white shirts and trousers with a black necktie. I had a white shirt but Mom had to take me downtown to be fitted for the trousers and purchase a black tie.

I remember leaving the house that afternoon wearing that white outfit, feeling extremely self-conscious and conspicuous, hoping no one was looking. I kept my head down as I hurried along Whitelaw Avenue, afraid if I looked up, I'd see someone who knew me.

I don't remember too much about the ceremony. It seemed to take forever to hand diplomas to one hundred and forty-nine kids. As it turned out, it was not just our eighth grade, it was all eighth grade graduates in the district.

After we had received our diplomas, we had to assemble for a group picture. I was up in the middle and almost lost behind another boy that was slightly taller. I just happened to peek around his head as the picture was taken.

After the ceremony, I left school as fast as I could and hurried home to take off that white outfit. I eventually wore out the white shirt or outgrew it, and probably wore the tie a few times, but the pants hung in the closet, never to be wore again.

School was finally out and I had graduated; something I had really doubted would happen when the school year had started. I felt pretty good about myself but knew it would never have happened if it hadn't been for the confidence building and support provided by Miss Stevenson. I've always been sorry that over the years I never made time to visit her and let her know how she affected and inspired one boy. But that was behind me now and three months of summer vacation lay ahead.

I was working evenings but I had all my days free to do as I pleased. The summer of 1944 was spent much like all past summers—swimming, hiking, and camping out occasionally.

During that summer, Billy Shockley, my cousin from Olive Branch came up to spend some time with us. It was while he was there that we planned another overnight camp-out in the woods on the hill behind the cemetery.

There were six boys in the group, me, Marvin, Jack, Billy, and our other two cousins, Tommy Lawrence and Bobby Worthington.

We all assembled at our house in the afternoon and hiked up over the hill toward the woods. When we got to the large lone oak tree at the top, we sat down and rested, and someone suggested that we camp right there. It was a great campsite and we had just about decided upon it when Marvin pointed out that it was too public; everyone in East Alton and Wood River would see our campfire.

The spot we eventually settled on was back in the woods, on a ridge that had three trails converging, and only about a hundred yards from our favorite grapevine swings.

After spending the remaining daylight hours swinging on the vines and running all over the woods like Indians, we settled down and started preparing our campsite for the night.

While a couple of us got a fire started, the rest gathered as much firewood as they could, knowing we would be sitting around the campfire telling ghost stories most of the night.

Our evening meal consisted of the usual – hotdogs and roasted marshmallows—after which we sat around the fire on our bedrolls talking and cutting up. It was shortly after Marvin had told the ghost story of "Bloodybones," that he and I concocted a prank to pull on the others.

He had an old white sheet that he had rolled up in a tight ball and hid under his shirt. At an opportune moment he was going to slip out of camp without being seen, then creep back up one of the trails and act like a ghost. He probably wouldn't be missed with so many boys moving around, talking, or staring into the campfire and also it was rather difficult to see what was happening just a few feet away from the circle of light.

As Marvin started to ease back into the woods, Jack evidently heard him and looked around. I immediately put my finger to my mouth to silence him. We started talking louder to cover any sounds that Marvin might make while slipping away.

This now meant that Billy, Tommy and Bobby were totally unaware of what was about to happen. After Marvin had been gone for a few minutes I kept glancing toward the trails, trying to see any movement on the trail he would be using. Billy had been up and down getting more wood for the fire and had just turned to pick up another stick of wood as this large white ghostly figure started walking toward him. Billy caught the movement out of the corner of his eye as he straightened up. He stood frozen, staring at the large white ghost-like glob gliding up the path toward him. He hesitated momentarily then raised the stick in his hand and with a frightened croaky voice said, "Get out of here!" Marvin, fearing he was about to get whopped with a club, threw the sheet in the air and screamed real loud. Billy went about a foot in the air as well as the rest of us, even though we knew what was happening.

I don't think Billy thought it was very funny at the time, but we all got a big laugh out of it. The remainder of the night was anticlimactic after Marvin's little stunt. We continued to sit around the campfire talking until well past midnight, and then tried to settle down and sleep. Notice, I said tried; we rarely slept very soundly on these outings and by daylight we were always ready to give it up and drag ourselves home.

Chapter XXIX

The Conspiracy

Because of the labor shortage throughout the country, many women were now working in defense plants. The women living in our housing complex were no different. Many of the mothers of our friends were working at the Western Cartridge Company, located about one mile away in Alton. Because we kids were now big enough to take care of ourselves, Mom decided she too should pitch-in and do her patriotic duty.

During that summer, Mom and Aunt Wave hired on at Western, becoming among the employed. I know this was a great diversion for them. After all the years of staying home and raising children, the hustle and bustle of a defense factory had to be an exciting change. Mom had worked in a hat factory in St. Louis before she married and was not unfamiliar to factory work.

I spent most of that summer in the Wood River swimming pool. Occasionally Monty and I would head for the woods or one of the ponds to try and outsmart those sun perch and catfish. During these sorties, our trusty BB guns were usually with us, although quite often we would now take Monty's 22 cal rifle with us.

During that summer we also became very interested in the game of billiards. Of course, we called it pool, regardless of what game we played. Gene Fitch, my friend who lived in the unit next to ours, acquainted us with Yoder's Tavern and Pool Hall in East Alton. The pool hall was separate from the tavern and we would go there quite frequently in the evening and play pool and drink Pepsi-Cola.

We would frequent a small restaurant just a few doors up the street from Yoder's after we finished playing pool. I don't remember its name, but I'll never forget it because it was outside this café that I got sick the first time from smoking a cigarette.

Marvin, Monty and I were standing on the sidewalk after just leaving the café, when we decided to smoke a cigarette. Thinking we were big stuff, we stood there trying to be nonchalant with the cigarette dangling from our lips while talking, like Humphrey Bogart did in the movies, trying not to choke or cough when we inhaled.

I was only about half way through my cigarette when I suddenly started feeling a little queasy. I didn't know how Monty or Marvin was doing and was not about to admit I was getting sick, so I kept smoking, but the puffs were becoming less frequent.

It hit me all of a sudden and I became so sick I thought I was going to die, and then I was afraid that I wouldn't. Whatever front I was trying to put on was now gone and within a minute or two I became so dizzy I had to squat down and lean against the wall of the café to keep from losing my balance. I was eventually down on my hands and knees on the sidewalk moaning and groaning.

About fifteen minutes later I was still alive and my head was starting to clear. As Marvin and Monty stood by, I told them that it was passing and I'd be OK in a few minutes. It would probably have been a blessing if that cigarette sickness had lasted longer; if so, no one could have withstood it long enough to acquire the habit. I did eventually acquire the habit and continued to smoke for a few years, but finally gave them up for good, while in the service. I'll admit that it was probably the hardest thing I ever did.

My sisters, Rita and Norma, pulled their own little stunt while we lived in East Alton. Dad had given Rita and Norma the money to go to the movie show, but Mom was against them walking all the way to the theater. Dad thought it would be all right, so Mom relented and let them go. It could have also been because our Aunt Norma and Uncle Bill Robinson were supposed to arrive that day from Kansas City, and she needed them out of the way to get ready for company.

Norma, although still very crippled from the effects of polio, could get around in her braces quite well without her wheelchair and walked just about anywhere she wanted. She was extremely independent and determined and never let infirmity get in her way.

The picture that was playing at the time that they were so anxious to see was "My Darling Clementine."

When they arrived at the theater they had to cross over from the opposite side of the street. There was a subway that ran under the road just a little farther up the street and Rita suggested they use it. Norma, always in a hurry, insisted that she could get across without any trouble and started across the street. Rita could see the car coming and screamed, " Come back! Come back!" but Norma ignored her and the car made contact with her just before it came to a screeching stop.

The bumper of the car struck Norma on the leg with the hip length brace and threw her to the curb. The ridged brace is actually what saved her from serious injuries.

Half scared out of his wits the driver jumped from the car and ran around to where Norma lay crying. He yelled, "Why are you crying?" "Where are you hurt, where are you hurt?"

Except for the bleeding scrapes to her nose and knee she wasn't. She told him she was crying because she had lost her movie money, the coins that she had been holding in her hand were jarred loose and had rolled down the drainage grates at the edge of the curb. The man immediately reached in his pocket and pulled out a roll of bills and shoved them into her hands.

The driver, rightly so, was really frightened and wanted her to see a doctor, but Norma refused. She also wouldn't give the man her name because she didn't want Mom to find out, especially after Mom had not wanted them to go in the first place.

With her nose and knees still bleeding, they hurried inside the theater to get away from the driver of the car, who was probably concerned that he would be in serious trouble if he didn't see that she received medical attention.

As they sat in the theater, Rita, who had been more frightened than Norma, continued to berate her for not listening to her in the first place when she wanted to go through the subway. Norma sat there sniffling because the abrasions were starting to burn as she continued to daub at them with her dress tail.

They soon realized they had another problem, how were they going to explain all that money that the driver of the car had given them. They knew they couldn't hide it without Mom finding out about it eventually, so they came up with the best idea they could think of – spend it.

Rita went back and forth to the concession stand to buy whatever they could think of. Thank goodness they were having a double feature. When the movie was over, they stopped at the same little café where I had gotten so sick from smoking and continued to try to spend the rest. They literally stuffed themselves with all the candy, ice cream, and soda pop they could hold. By the time they left for home, they were sick.

When they arrived home Aunt Norma, Mom's sister, and Uncle Bill were there. Their car was parked in front of the building. At first they were afraid to go in with Norma all skinned up; they knew Mom would be very upset and would probably not let them go to the theater by themselves again.

They devised a plan in which Rita would go in first and keep them occupied while Norma slipped past and went to the bathroom to clean up and remove as much dried blood as possible.

Rita went through the door and immediately ran to our Aunt and started hugging her. But it didn't work. Our Aunt turned and saw Norma Fern coming through the door and yelled with a her booming voice, "Norma! What happened to you?" Everyone jerked their heads in Norma's direction and Mom asked in a disgusted, yet concerned manner, "Well, Norma Fern, what happened to you, hon?"

Norma's explanation that her appearance was due to her falling against the curb was not entirely untrue and served to satisfy everyone's curiosity for the moment.

By the next day Rita and Norma were starting to relax a little and were just about convinced that the incident was forgotten and would have been, I suppose, if it had not been for the concern and guilty conscience of the driver of the car.

The day following Norma's accident, Gene Fitch and I were playing marbles just outside our bedroom window, between the building and Whitelaw Avenue. We gave no notice of the car that pulled up beside us until the driver leaned out the window and asked, "Do you boys know a girl that lives around here who wears braces and was hit by a car yesterday?"

We looked at each other and I hesitated a moment before saying, "No, we didn't know anyone got hit by a car!" Of course I knew Norma was all skinned up but neither she nor Rita had confided in any of us. I then turned and looked toward the bedroom window where Norma had been standing watching us play marbles. She had moved back from the window and was standing there shaking her head at me vigorously. I quickly turned back to the man and said, "No one around here was hit by a car." The man sat there for a few seconds looking around as if trying to decide what to do next, then said thanks, and slowly drove south on Whitelaw, looking around as he went.

After he drove out of sight, I immediately went in the house and entered the bedroom and asked, "OK Nonk," her nick name, "What's going on?" She then told the whole story of what had happened the day before. The only permanent damage was a small dent in the side of Norma's leg brace. I've wondered over the years, how long it took before that driver felt secure that the police was not going to come and knock upon his door? It was many years before Mom learned the truth about this incident.

My summer vacation passed much too fast that year. It seemed as if it only lasted a few weeks. Of course, I had been noticing for some time that each summer vacation was becoming shorter than the previous one. I suppose this was a sign of growing up; putting time in its proper perspective.

My first day of high school, I believe it was September 4, 1944, was one big confusing day. Instead of staying in one classroom, I had to locate different rooms for different subjects, each time detouring to my locker to change textbooks.

Monty was still living in Roxana school district and was attending Roxana High School. Although we still got together fairly regularly, especially on weekends, it was Howard Buckner that I chummed around with while attending Wood River High.

I had known Howard for many years because we attended the same church. Prior to high school, I believe he had attended school in the Hartford school district.

We had only been in school a week when they came around signing up boys for the freshmen football team. Now this was more like it; maybe this high school wasn't going to be so bad after all.

I remember the day we went to the gym to be issued our uniforms. The coach threw out different sizes of articles in little piles. It was evident that the uniforms had seen better days. The uniform I ended up with was big and baggy and the belt had no buckle, so I had to tie it. The pants filled out a little after I shoved the thigh pads into position. The color of the pants was somewhere between brown and mustard yellow.

I'm not sure what the shoulder and hip pads were made of, but I believe it was some sort of Bakelite material that made an awfully loud clacking noise when hit or slapped. The helmet was made of hard perforated leather with thick solid strips crisscrossing the top; a far cry from the high-tech uniforms of today. Of course, for the times, we thought we were in high fashion.

I believe the freshmen football team never lost a game that year. I remember playing several positions, full back and guard, although I was very light for both of those positions. There were no specialties in those days. Most players played offense and defense according to wherever they were needed a body to plug a hole.

I remember two games very distinctly—the Western Military Academy, which we played in Alton and Roxana, played in Wood River.

After school the team piled onto a bus, fully uniformed, and headed for Alton. When we arrived at the Academy, we unloaded right onto the football field. The Academy had not fielded their team and we had it all to ourselves as we began warming up and practicing.

When the Academy football team came running onto the field with their pretty bright blue uniforms, they looked like giants, and I believe on the average they were probably larger than our team. Some members of our team, and probably me as well, were making remarks about how big they were when the coach looked at us and said, "Well, what do you want to do, get back on the bus and go home?" That did it, we were now fighting-mad.

I found myself playing offensive line against a boy that I knew out weighed me by at least twenty pounds and that bright blue uniform made him look twice as big.

He was down on point across from me, teeth clinched, lips pulled back, and growling at me like a mad dog. He just about had me convinced that I was about to die, when our quarterback hiked the ball. I stiffened out and shot forward and hit him around the thighs and he just rolled over my back. I was up and looking for someone else to block before he was able to get to his feet. The next couple of plays ended the same way. Each time when he landed upon the ground his whole body wabbled like Jell-O. I guess I was doing pretty well that day because the coach gave me more playing time during that game than any other.

The team I was really looking forward to playing was Roxana, because Monty was playing on that team in their backfield. I was hoping I'd get one crack at him sometime during the game.

We were on the field when the Roxana team bus pulled in. I watched to make sure Monty was with the team. We left the field to them for a short practice session and then the game started. I was not one of the starters, but I knew I would be in there eventually.

The first time the coach sent me in was on offense. It was during the second quarter that I finally got my opportunity. I'd been standing on the sideline chomping at the bit to get into the game before Monty was pulled out of the game, when the coach said, "Get in there Isom."

I'd been in for a couple of plays and Monty and I had been looking back and forth at each other. He knew I was just waiting for him to carry the ball. Finally Monty got the ball and swung around the end and I scooted down the line keeping Monty in front of me as he came forward. I broke through and caught him full force and we went down with me on top.

As I knelt over him lying flat on his back, I said, "Gotcha!" He opened his eyes and for the first time recognized who had tackled him. We got up, slapped each other on the back and hurriedly returned to our respective huddles. This was probably the most memorable play of my entire football career. Of course this was nothing new for Monty and me. We had been tackling each other for years in our sandlot football games.

Except for the normal amount of fat lips, bloody noses (no face guards in those days), bloody knuckles, and numerous scratches, I only had one injury that really caused me any lasting pain. It was a bruise on my hipbone.

When football ended, so did my enthusiasm for school. I just couldn't bring myself to overcome my aversion to the drudgery of the classroom. It was probably the English class that I dreaded most. I didn't mind reading literature but I hated making book reports and especially when they had to be given orally.

It was much later in life that I began to realize the importance of being able to express yourself in front of an audience. I'm sure there have been many brilliant careers that were stunted because of this inability, but in 1944, all the English teachers and public speaking teachers in the State of Illinois could not have convinced me of that.

My mind was too preoccupied in 1944 with the world around me to be interested in school studies. I would rather be reading war news than studying history. I would rather be in the woods and fields hunting, fishing and experiencing it, than studying science or geography, and I'd much rather be working and making money than studying English Literature in a classroom.

It would be many years before I would really understand the real meaning of freedom and the relationship between it and education. I would come to learn that true freedom was the freedom to choose and the options to choose increase with education.

Winter came and with it the joy of Christmas. I would always look forward to the Christmas season and even as I grew older, my enthusiasm for it never diminished. I enjoyed walking along downtown Ferguson Avenue where the street and stores were all decorated for the holidays. But the spirit of Christmas just didn't last long enough. After the first of January the winter blues would set in and I would impatiently wait for the first signs of spring.

Chapter XXX

At That Moment, I Was Huck

The one big diversion from the doldrums of winter was the news coming from all theaters of war and it was mostly good. On New Years Day, 1945, we received news that the German Luftwaffe lost over two hundred aircraft in attacks over Belgium and Holland. On January 6, the Japanese lost seventy-five Kamikaze planes on the ground in Luzon to American land and carrier based forces.

Also in January came the news of the invasion of Luzon in the Philippines and the opening of the Burma Road by convoy led by General "Vinegar Joe" Stilwell.

Our one big loss came in March when we learned that eight hundred thirty-five sailors were killed during a Kamikaze attack against the aircraft carrier Franklin, the highest casualties ever suffered by an American carrier during the war.

At home, on March 15, the Academy Award for best picture for 1944, went to "Going My Way." Bing Crosby also won Best Actor for the same picture.

On April 12, 1945, Franklin D. Roosevelt, our thirty-second President died in Warm Springs, Georgia. Regardless of one's political persuasion at the time, his passing was mourned by a whole nation. He was the only President to be elected four times, but lived to serve only about two and one half months of his fourth term.

*   *   *

It was on a Saturday during the month of March, after coming from a Saturday matinee movie at the Alton Theater, that Howard Buckner and I went down to the riverfront. This was almost a ritual with us boys. I can hardly recall a time visiting Alton without walking down to the locks.

We could stay there for hours watching one boat after the other, "lock through." The clanging noise of cables and ratchets coming into contact with the steel decks; the constant rumbling of the big engines and the smell of diesel fuel; watching the water rush in and out of the locks as the boats would rise and fall, all added to the excitement and mystery of the river boating.

The railing where we stood was only about ten feet from the boats as they passed through. We were always curious as to where they had come from and where they were going. If one of the deck hands would pass by close enough we would ask. Many of them were teenagers no older than we were and always willing to talk.

The destinations of these towboats, a misnomer by the way, would be heading just about anywhere the rivers were navigable, and that was just about anywhere in the eastern half of the United States. Those traveling down river were usually empty or carrying very light cargo and were coming from the Minneapolis/St. Paul area or had come down the Illinois River from as far as Chicago or the Great Lakes. Those going up river may have come from as far away as Port Arthur, Texas, Pittsburgh, Pennsylvania, or had just loaded their barges with gasoline from the Wood River dock about five miles down river.

Sometimes we would be lucky enough to catch a boat of war going down river, such as a LST, (Landing Ship Tank) a large landing craft for troops and cargo, a Liberty ship (Cargo Ship), or sometimes we would really get excited when a submarine came through.

Those long low-silhouetted boats, painted black, with sailors standing in their conning towers, were awesome. We would stand staring wide-eyed, our minds conjuring up all kinds of images from the stories we had heard, or war movies we had watched.

There was so much going on in the world around me at that time I could not maintain any degree of concentration on my studies or activities in the classroom. Although I attended regularly, I may as well not have been there as far as classroom participation was concerned. I don't even think the teachers knew I was there.

Howard and I had fantasized about working on the river for sometime, however, that was all it was, just a fantasy. We never thought that we would really do it. On several weekends we went down to the Wood River dock to watch the activity and look at the different boats docked there.

It was probably the second or third weekend that we had spent at the docks when we started seriously thinking about actually working on the river. We decided it was something we really wanted to do but still doubted that we ever would. Even if we did decide to go to work on a river boat we would have to wait until we were sixteen, and that would be another five months for me and Howard was about the same age.

It was one Sunday morning while attending Sunday school that Howard and I made up our minds that we would really try to get a job on the river. We didn't know if they would hire us because of our age, but, if necessary, we would lie and say we were. Surely no one would ask to see a birth certificate if they really needed help very badly.

We were going to wait until the following Saturday before we made our move. In the meantime I started planning for the eventuality of actually leaving home and going to work on the river. The first step was to clue Marvin in on what Howard and I were planning. I knew I could count on Marvin to assist me in any way he could and to keep it quiet from Mom and Dad. If they knew what I was up to, they would never allow it.

By Friday, Howard and I were in a high state of anxiety and agitation that had been building all week. We had allowed ourselves to become convinced that Friday would be our last day of school. We were so convinced that we would be hired on Saturday that we had already packed and hidden our clothes for a fast getaway.

As it turned out we never waited until Saturday. It was at the end of our English class, the first period after lunch that the decision was made for us. Just before class was dismissed the teacher had assigned us another one of those dumb book reports. That did it...

When Howard and I left the classroom and walked down the hall to our lockers, we decided that we would leave right then. I don't know who hated book reports more, him or me, but we both knew she wouldn't be receiving one from us.

We opened our lockers and threw our books in, locked them, and walked out the south entrance that faced the football field and headed for the Wood River docks.

I can remember our excitement as well as a high degree of apprehension as we hurried along toward the docks. Even though we may not have expressed it to each other, we knew we had committed ourselves to whatever lay ahead. We knew that the least that would happen would be having to explain skipping class if our plan didn't work. If on the other hand we were hired, then that would be a problem we wouldn't have to worry about.

Our biggest fear as we neared the docks was that there would be no boats, as sometimes happened. As we walked along the gravel road leading down to the river we could see the stacks of at least one boat. We knew then that we had at least one chance so we both crossed our fingers.

When we got nearer we could see that it was one that we had never seen before. It looked about as wide as it was long, painted mostly white with black on the bottom half of each deck. "Vagabond" was its name.

We walked down the bank a short distance and sat down on a couple of large rocks lining the bank to watch and build up our courage before going aboard to ask for a job. We noticed there was very little activity on the boat, but the tankermen, a title that I would later learn, were busy on the barges as they were being loaded with gasoline.

Occasionally an older man would walk out onto the deck of the boat, piddle around, and then walk back in. We couldn't tell if he was someone of authority but decided we would ask him if they were looking for help.

We were real nervous as we boldly walked aboard the Vagabond, expecting any moment to hear, "You kids get the hell off this boat!" But that didn't happen. Suddenly the man we had seen before appeared around the corner, he looked to be about fifty years old. He smiled and said "Hello," and about the same time, because of my nervousness I blurted out, "We're looking for a job."

The man, without looking us up or down or being judgmental in any way, casually said, "Well, we're looking for help, but you'll have to talk with the captain." He asked us to follow him and led us up to the pilothouse and introduced us to him.

Captain Sullivan was a man in his late thirties or early forties with a medium build and red hair. At first we were very uncomfortable standing there in front of him. He was sitting in a tall chair in front of the control panel, slowly swiveling back and forth looking at us curiously. He suddenly asked, "How old are you boys?" In unison we both said "sixteen." He let that go without comment, then asked if we had any experience. Of course we didn't and there was no way to lie about that so again in unison we answered "No."

The next thing he said made my heart skip a beat. Could this be for real? Did he really mean it? Was he actually asking us when we could start? "Right now," we both blurted out, not realizing how desperate and anxious we both probably sounded. He then said, "We're coupling up and pulling out this evening, as soon as we're loaded. Can you be back with your gear by then?"

No matter how grown up and professional I tried to act, I couldn't keep the silly grin off my face. In fact, that silly grin probably stayed on my face for the next couple days.

After we had told him we could be back within two hours or probably sooner, we took off for home as fast as we could. We didn't realize it at the time, but we were probably functioning under a mild case of shock. We kept up a constant line of chatter while walking and running all the way home, neither hearing much of what the other was saying.

I had about a mile farther to go than Howard. He lived west of Wood River Avenue and I had to go all the way to East Alton.

When I finally got home and went in the house, I tried not to act too excited as I motioned Marvin to follow me to the bedroom. After I had closed the bedroom door I busted out grinning again and told Marvin that I was leaving for the river. He started grinning also and asked unbelievingly, "Really?" I then told him what Howard and I had done and that I had to leave right then and get back to the boat because we were leaving Wood River within a couple of hours. Marvin asked where we were going and I just looked at him kind of dumb, then said "I don't know." That was the first time the thought had occurred to me. Of course, it didn't really matter.

I opened the bedroom window and removed the screen, then lowered my clothes bag to the ground. After closing the window, Marvin and I wandered nonchalantly back through the house and out the kitchen door. We walked around to the end of the house where I had placed my bag. We stood there for only a minute or two, because I had to get back to the river as fast as I could, then we shook hands and I took off.

I was about a block down Whitelaw before I turned and looked back. Marvin was still standing there with his hands in his pockets watching me go. I waved one more time and then turned and never looked back again.

I'm sure I covered the three miles or so back to the dock in record time. When I arrived at the boat Howard was already there. The older gentleman that we had met turned out to be the first mate. He had already shown Howard where we would be bunking and I put my gear in the cabin with his.

The cabin was very austere. The deck, overhead, and bulkheads were all steel. It was about ten feet by ten feet with one window. Below the window was a small desk and chair. Along each side were double bunks with metal lockers at the end of each bunk. The bulkheads were freshly painted white and the deck battleship gray.

Of course at the moment I didn't care what anything looked like – it was a boat, I was on it, and that was all that mattered.

We were still in the process of stowing our gear when the first mate stuck his head in the door and said, "All right, let's go to work." It was only then that Howard and I realized just how desperate they really were for help. Beside the first mate, Howard and I made up the entire deck crew.

The rest of the crew was made up of the two pilots, of whom one was Captain Sullivan, the cook, two engineers, and three tankermen, that stayed in a little cabin on each barge, but ate their meals on board the boat.

When it came time to make tow, as it's called, everyone pitched in except the cook and the engineers. Howard and I were green as gourds and had to be shown every little task. The first mate who reminded me of an old farmer, which he was, was very patient with our fumbling and ineptness, but we soon had it all coupled and ready to go.

As we were preparing to cast off, the mate asked us if we had a preference of watches. Although we had heard the phrase mentioned in the movies, we had no idea how it worked. He explained that a watch was a work shift. There were two watches, the forward watch and the after watch. He assigned Howard the forward watch. He would work until midnight and I would relieve him and work until six o'clock in the morning. Then he would relieve me. It was six hours on and six hours off continuously.

The three big diesels started churning as we pulled away from the dock. There was no way I could possibly sleep. I was so revved up with adrenaline at that moment that a dozen sleeping pills would not have put me down.

As the string of barges swung out into midstream I hurried to the fantail to watch the churning of the cloudy water as the big screws worked fiercely beneath my feet. I stood there for the longest, watching Wood River dock slowly disappear.

While standing there I wondered how many boys that I had grown up with would give anything to be in my shoes at that moment. Little did I realize at that very moment that my childhood had ended. I didn't realize it at the time, but never again would I fish Boman's pond, or hike the woods at Vaughn's or Ninth Street Hill, or hunt turtles and fish for crawdads in Grassy Lake. I would never again dance with the girls at Jive-Land or swim in the Wood River pool, and little did I know that it would be many years before I would again return to the only hometown I'd ever known.

I took one more quick look in the direction of Wood River, then turned my back and hurried toward the bow. I went to the lounge deck and leaned at the railing looking ahead. With the wind in my face, my hair and shirt blowing,

I looked over and beyond the marker flag at the head of the barges as it slowly inched across the landscape ahead. As the barges slowly swung westward, the only thing I could see ahead was a future of excitement and adventure. My heart was truly full. At that moment, I was Huck.

Epilogue

We know the ending of a book is never really the end, especially in a biography covering only the early years. There is much yet to be said about the author's family and the boys of Halloran Avenue. Their lives did not end with the author's departure from Wood River, Illinois in 1945. To the contrary, with the exception of the author's father, most went on to live relatively long and successful lives.

The following is a short biography of many mentioned within the pages of Huckleberry Heart, starting with members of the author's family.

John Nelson Isom, the author's father, retired from the Shell Oil Company in 1945 and moved the family to Olive Branch, Illinois. He returned to Wood River in early 1947 to work at his old job at the Shell Oil Refinery. He died of pneumonia there in October 1947.

Dorothy Mildred Irey Isom, the author's mother, eventually married Mr. Leon Sams of Olive Branch, Illinois and remained very active within her church, teaching Sunday school for many years. She continued to write and stay mentally alert and active until her death at the age of 97. She was living with her daughter, Rita, at the time of her death on December 8, 1999.

Marvin Isom joined the Army Air Corps in 1946 and became an aircraft mechanic. He served as a crewmember on B-29 aircraft during his enlistment, spending most of his enlistment in Japan. After his discharge from the Air Corps, he attended Parks College for a while, and then transferred to Southeast Missouri State at Cape Girardeau, Missouri. He left there after about a year and started a sawmill business. With limited business, he gave up and went to work for MacDonnell Douglas Aircraft Company in St. Louis, Missouri where he remained for over thirty-eight years. He married Louise Bridges, of Olive Branch, Illinois and they had two sons, four grandchildren and two great grandchildren. Marvin was eventually forced to retire due to poor health. He finally succumbed to serious arthritis and heart failure, just a few days short of his sixty-ninth birthday in 1997.

Rita Isom married Maurice Browning of Olive Branch, Illinois in 1948. They had three sons, one daughter, several grandchildren and great grandchildren. They remained in Olive Branch with the exception of her husband serving two enlistments in the army. During his time in the army, they served at Fort Knox, Kentucky, Fort Lee, Virginia and Japan. Maurice died in 1991 and Rita still maintains her home in Olive Branch, but spends time with her son in Alaska and her daughter in Terra Haute, Indiana.

Norma Isom, after graduating from Thebes, Illinois High School, attended Southeast Missouri State University for a time before she married. She and her husband Orman Winn lived in Elgin, Illinois while he worked for Eastern Airlines and Norma worked for United Airlines. Orman transferred with the airlines to Tampa, Florida where they remained until his retirement. Orman died in 2004 and Norma still spends the winter months at Lake Wales, Florida with her children—one son, two daughters, grandchildren and great grandchildren—but returns to her home in Olive Branch, Illinois from April through November.

Jack Isom joined the Navy in 1951 and he, like his brothers, became an aircraft mechanic and served in San Diego, California, Guam and Japan. After his discharge from the service, he married Betty Caldwell of Thebes, Illinois and they had two sons, four granddaughters and one grandson. Both sons earned their degrees from Southeast Missouri State University at Cape Girardeau. The oldest recently retired from the army with the rank of Colonel and his youngest is an executive with a firm in Huntsville, Alabama. Jack entered civil service and eventually worked his way up through the executive service. He earned a Bachelor degree from the University of Oklahoma, Norman. At the time of his retirement, he was a Senior Executive at the Redstone Arsenal at Huntsville, Alabama. Jack and his wife, Marcia, belong to the Valley Hill Country Club, play golf, travel and are fully enjoying their retirement.

Tommy Lawrence left Wood River High School in 1947 just two months before graduation, to take a full-time job as produce manager in a Kroger

Store, after serving as a night manager in a drug store for several months. He later graduated from Waynesville, Missouri High School in 1950. He was drafted in the army in 1950. He spent his tour of duty at Fort Leonard Wood, Missouri. He married Helen Greyson of Wood River and they had one son, one daughter, five grandchildren and seven great grandchildren. He worked for the Shell Oil Refinery for twenty-eight years and was supervising the Electrical Engineering Design Department at the time of his retirement. After his active duty with the army, he continued his military career in the Army Reserve and retired with the rank of Lieutenant Colonel. Tommy continued his education throughout his life and earned a Bachelor of Arts degree in mathematics with minors in physics and economics. He attended night school at St. Louis University for his M.B.A. He eventually earned his PhD in Industrial Management. Tommy later married Bonnie Goode and they are now fully retired and reside in Dorsey, Illinois.

Jack Stahlheber graduated from Wood River-East Alton High School in January 1945 and served in the U.S. Navy from 1945 through 1946, attaining the rank of Yeoman 3rd Class. After his military service, he attended Washington University, St. Louis before transferring to DePauw University in Greencastle, Indiana and graduated in 1950 with an BA degree in Economics, then on to Illinois State at Normal, Illinois where he earned his teaching credentials. Jack eventually earned his M.B.A. while attending City University, Seattle, Washington. He taught 6th grade at the Milton School in Alton, Illinois from 1951 through 1953 before working in an actuary department with an insurance company and finished out his professional career working as an Estimating and Job Planner with three commercial printing firms. He retired in March of 1991. He married Elizabeth Carle of Chicago, Illinois in 1955. They have two daughters and four grandchildren. Jack and Elizabeth now live in Redmond, Washington and are spending their retirement years traveling, gardening and playing golf.

Ben Stahlheber graduated from the East Alton-Wood River, Illinois High School in 1947 and attended the University of Illinois, initially at the extension in Galesburg, then moved to the main campus at Champaign-Urbana and graduated with a B.S. degree in Electrical Engineering in 1952. He married Ruth Audrey Williams, of Roxana, Illinois in 1952 and they now have one daughter, two sons, one granddaughter and three grandsons. Throughout his career, Ben worked on more than 800 lighting design projects in the U.S. and Canada. He was a Visiting Lecturer in lighting for graduate architect students at Yale, Pennsylvania, Princeton, and Rhode Island School of Design. He became a registered Professional Engineer in five states and in D.C. He also was co-inventor of several lighting luminaires for which they received patents. Ben has been a member of the Illuminating Engineering Society of North America since 1954. He and Ruth have settled down in Clinton, Connecticut and have been enjoying their retirement since 2000.

Herb Paton's family moved from Alton, Illinois to 811 Halloran Avenue, Wood River, Illinois in 1928 when Herb was only eighteen months old. His family, maintained the home at that address until it was sold in 1966. Herb and his bother Bob, both became Eagle Scouts in 1941. Herb skipped his final senior semester in the fall of 1944 and entered Shurtleff College for a time before joining the Navy. After completing his Navy enlistment, he attended DePauw University in Indiana and graduated in 1950, majoring in physics and math and completed a long successful career in sales management of electronic instrumentation and controls for electric power and industrial manufacturing processes. He married Sue Bennett of Medina, Ohio in 1953. They have three daughters, three sons, eleven granddaughters, four grandsons and one great grandson. Herb and Sue have retired to a retirement community in Green Valley, Arizona; where he regularly plays tennis. He and Sue both are very active in their church missions.

Jean Paton graduated from high school in 1941 and from Shurtleff College in 1945 with a degree in music. She received a four-year fellowship for training in voice, opera and classical music at the Julliard Graduate School of Music in New York City. She was a member and soloist with the Robert Shaw Chorale, performing at Carnegie Hall several time, in many cities on national concert tours, and recorded several Victor Red Seal albums with Toscanini directing the NBC Symphony Orchestra. She married Patrick Warren, of New York City in 1960 and has one daughter. She is widowed and lives near Albany, NY where she still sings weekly for her church.

Robert (Bob) Paton graduated from high school in 1943, served in the Pacific Theater as an Air Corp Gunner and graduated from Illinois State University. He married JoAnne Stoltz of Kankakee, Illinois in 1952 and was an executive with both the Boy Scouts and the Girl Scout in Illinois, Indiana and Iowa. They have four sons and nine grandchildren. Since retirement, he has lived near Crossville, Tennessee where he is an avid golfer.

The author's sidekick, Monty Heffner, joined the army right out of the Roxana, Illinois High School. After completing basic training, he spent the remainder of his enlistment in Japan and attained the rank of sergeant. After completing his military service, he married Virginia Steffen of Roxana, Illinois. He had one daughter, two sons and six grandchildren. He spent thirty years as a pipe fitter for the Shell oil refinery in Roxana, Illinois before retiring in 1988. Monty married Irene Pruitt of Alton, Illinois in 1979. He remained the consummate outdoorsman throughout his life, although the environs of his old haunts were now gone. Houses, large buildings and asphalt exists where he and Gene once patrolled the woods and fields to protect the realm with their Daisy Red Riders. Monty left us in May of 2003, but we know that his spirit lives on in every young boy who fishes in a pond, or hunts in a wooded lot. Wherever these young adventurers gather, we know that Monty is there.

The author, after throwing his books in his locker and walking out the back door of the Wood River high School in 1945, spent the next year as a deck hand on towboats. He traveling the main waterways of the Eastern United States; up the Mississippi River from Wood River to Minneapolis, to New Orleans and on over to Port Arthur, Texas on the inter-coastal waterway, Up the Ohio River as far as Pittsburgh and the Illinois River to Chicago. He intends to make a sequel titled "Huckleberry Heart on The River." In the summer of 1946, he worked for a time with the Dyer's Greater Shows, a carnival, traveling throughout Illinois and Iowa. He worked as a farm hand during that fall while waiting for his seventeenth birthday, and joined the Army on January 4, 1947. He spent seven years in the army, serving in Hawaii, Korea, Japan and California. He attained the rank of TSgt at the time of his discharge. He returned home to Olive Branch and Married his hometown sweetheart, Doris Legg on April 10, 1954. They have one son, one daughter, five grandsons and one granddaughter. He later joined the Air Force and spent the next fourteen years with the Strategic Air Command, serving most of the time working the flight-line as a B-52 Crew Chief, Maintenance Planner and Scheduler and Flight Crew Debriefer. He retired with twenty-one years total military service. He spent the next twenty-one years with Eastern Air lines, serving in Tampa, Florida, St. Louis, Missouri and Gainesville, Florida. During his employment with Eastern Air lines, he worked in several areas within the department of Passenger-Services. After retiring from the Air Lines in 1990, he worked for a time as an Income Tax preparer. At the time of this writing, he and Doris have celebrated their fifty-second wedding anniversary. They are now fully retired and spend the spring and autumn months at their place on Horseshoe Lake in Olive Branch, Illinois. The author has written another book titled, "Tales of Pigeon Roost Hollow and More." He continues to write political essays and is planning several other projects, including co-Authoring a book with his wife Doris.